Microsoft® Excel 2002

fast&easy®

Check the Web for Updates

To check for updates or corrections relevant to this book and/or CD-ROM, visit our updates page on the Web at **http://www.prima-tech.com/support/**.

Send Us Your Comments

To comment on this book or any other PRIMA TECH title, visit our reader response page on the Web at **http://www.prima-tech.com/comments**.

How to Order

For information on quantity discounts, contact the publisher: Prima Publishing, P.O. Box 1260BK, Rocklin, CA 95677-1260; (916) 787-7000. On your letterhead, include information concerning the intended use of the books and the number of books you want to purchase. For individual orders, turn to the back of this book for more information.

Microsoft® Excel 2002
fast&easy®

Faithe Wempen

A DIVISION OF PRIMA PUBLISHING

A Division of Prima Publishing

Prima Publishing, colophon, and Fast & Easy are registered trademarks of Prima Communications, Inc. PRIMA TECH is a trademark of Prima Communications, Inc., Roseville, California 95661.

Publisher: Stacy L. Hiquet

Associate Marketing Manager: Heather Buzzingham

Managing Editor: Sandy Doell

Acquisitions Editor: Debbie Abshier

Project Editor: Kelly Talbot

Technical Reviewer: Natalie Houston

Copy Editor: Laura R. Gabler

Interior Layout: Marian Hartsough

Cover Design: Prima Design Team

Indexer: Sharon Hilgenberg

Proofreader: Jessica McCarty

ISBN: 0-7615-3398-2
Library of Congress Catalog Card Number: 2001086688
Printed in the United States of America

01 02 03 04 05 DD 10 9 8 7 6 5 4 3 2 1

To Margaret

Acknowledgments

Thanks once again to a great team at Prima for another good editorial experience. Kelly Talbot, project editor, managed the whole thing seamlessly from start to finish. Debbie Abshier, the best acquisitions editor in the business (ask anyone!), made the contractual and legal parts go painlessly. The book was truly a team effort.

About the Author

FAITHE WEMPEN owns and operates Your Computer Friend, a computer training and troubleshooting business in Indianapolis that specializes in helping individuals and small businesses with their PCs. She is also an A+ Certified computer technician with advanced training in computer hardware troubleshooting and repair. Faithe has an M.A. in English from Purdue University, where her area of specialty was Rhetoric and Composition. Her eclectic writing credits include more than 30 computer books, including *Upgrade Your PC in a Weekend* and *The Essential Excel 2000 Book*, as well as training manuals, OEM documentation, and magazine articles.

Contents at a Glance

Contents

Introduction

Excel 2002 is the most powerful and popular spreadsheet program in the world, and it contains several hundred features for data entry, formatting, calculation, and presentation. If that makes you a bit intimidated about jumping in, you're not alone. For people without a lot of experience in computing, learning a complex and powerful program like Excel can seem like a daunting task.

Fortunately, help is available. The Fast & Easy series from Prima Publishing tackles powerful programs like Excel from the very beginning. You learn individual tasks step-by-step, in a logical sequence that helps build skills and confidence. Because each step is fully illustrated, what you see in the book is exactly what you see on your own screen.

What Is Excel 2002?

Excel 2002 is a spreadsheet program. It's designed to display data in a grid of rows and columns onscreen and to print in the same type of neat row-and-column format. You can enter calculations called formulas that perform basic math operations such as adding or subtracting the values in two or more cells. You can also enter functions, which are shortcuts for more complex math operations such as averaging and calculating loan interest.

Excel 2002 can be purchased as a stand-alone product or as part of Microsoft Office XP, a suite of business programs. No matter how you have obtained Excel 2002, it functions the same way.

Who Should Read This Book?

This book starts at the no-experience-required level. If you are a beginner with computers or with the Windows environment, this book is perfect for you. It's also a great tool for those who might have used some other Microsoft Office product before, like Microsoft Word, but are new to Excel or to spreadsheets in general.

That doesn't mean, however, that this book covers only beginner-level topics. As you progress through the chapters, you'll be surprised at how much you are learning. By the end of the book, you will be proficient at some Excel skills that even the computer guru in your office might not be aware of.

How This Book Is Organized

Each chapter in the book covers a well-defined cluster of skills, such as file management or text formatting. A chapter consists of anywhere from three to six individual skills you can master, each fully illustrated.

Chapters are organized into small groups called parts. There are six regular parts in the book (the seventh contains appendices), and at the end of each part, you'll find ten review questions to help you test your understanding. If you have difficulty answering the questions, review the chapters and locate the answers before you move ahead.

In addition to the regular text in the chapter, you'll find notes and tips that point out shortcuts, background information, or suggestions for using the program in real-world ways.

Read and enjoy this Fast & Easy book. It is certainly the fastest and easiest way to learn Microsoft Excel 2002!

PART I

Building Your First Worksheet

1

Welcome to Excel 2002

Excel is a replacement for the accountant's columnar pad, sharp pencil, and calculator. However, you don't have to be an accountant to benefit from Excel. If you have complex calculations to figure out, Excel can handle them with ease. Yet even if your calculations are simple, Excel will make working with numbers fun and easy. The great thing about Excel is that you can present your data so that it has impact. You can create colorful charts, print transparencies or hard copy reports, add clip art and your company logo, and more! In this chapter, you'll learn how to:

- Start Excel 2002
- Enter text and numbers
- Move between cells
- Enter a simple formula
- Play "what if?"

Starting Excel

The Windows Start button is the easiest way to find your programs.

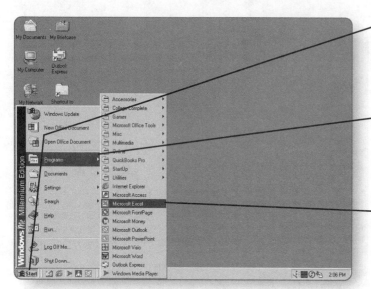

1. **Click** on the **Start button** on the Taskbar with the mouse button. A pop-up menu will appear.

2. **Move** the **mouse pointer** up the menu to Programs to highlight it. A second pop-up menu will appear.

3. **Move** the **mouse pointer** to the right and click on Microsoft Excel. The main Excel window will open.

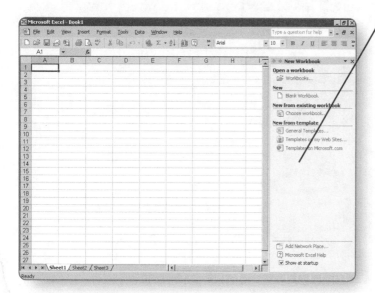

The task pane is a new element in Excel 2002. This pane provides shortcuts to common activities such as opening a saved workbook. You will learn more about it in Chapter 2.

NOTE

If Excel is not yet installed on your computer, see Appendix A.

Entering Text and Numbers

A *worksheet* is a rectangular grid of rows and columns. (Worksheets are also sometimes called *spreadsheets*; it's the same thing.) The columns are labeled with letters and the rows with numbers. The intersection of a row and a column is a *cell*. Each cell's address consists of the column letter followed by the row number. For example, cell C10 is at the intersection of column C and row 10.

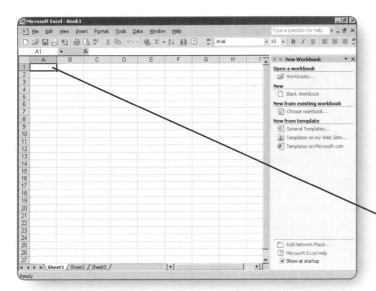

When you first open Excel, you'll notice that cell A1 has a border around it. This is the active cell.

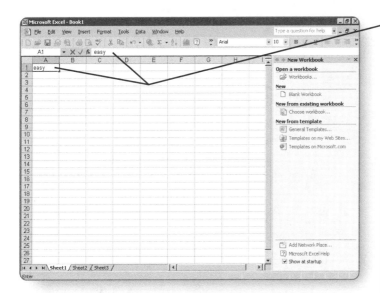

1. Type text in the active cell. A flashing insertion point will appear at the end of whatever you type. You'll notice that what you type will appear not only in the active cell but also in the formula bar.

NOTE

Text entries are called *labels*. Labels may contain any combination of letters, numbers, or symbols. Excel can only use numeric entries or values in a calculation. It cannot use labels.

2. Press the **Enter key**. The cell below the current active cell will become the new active cell.

The formula bar will be empty again because the new active cell is empty.

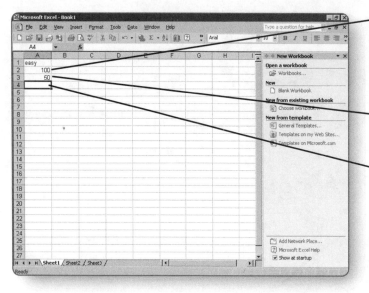

3. Type a **number** in A2.

4. Press the **Enter key**. Cell A3 will be highlighted.

5. Type a **different number** in A3.

6. Press the **Enter key**. Cell A4 will be highlighted.

Notice that Excel right aligns the number in the cell. Excel left aligns text but right aligns numbers. This makes viewing different types of data easier.

Moving Between Cells

There are several ways to navigate between cells.

The active cell is the one with the dark border around it, called the *cell cursor*. Anything you type goes into the active cell.

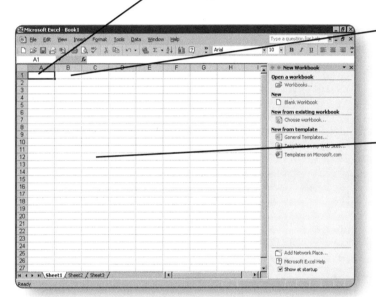

To move the cell cursor with the keyboard, use the arrow keys. For example, to move the cell cursor one column to the right, press the right arrow key once.

To move the cell cursor with the mouse, click on the cell you want. For example, to move the cell cursor to cell C12, click on that cell.

NOTE

There are also shortcuts for moving the cell cursor greater distances. See Appendix B for a complete list.

Entering a Formula

In this section, you will create a simple mathematical formula in a single cell, which adds two numbers together. First, make sure that the active cell is empty and located where you want the result of the formula to appear.

1. Type = (the equal sign) in cell A4.

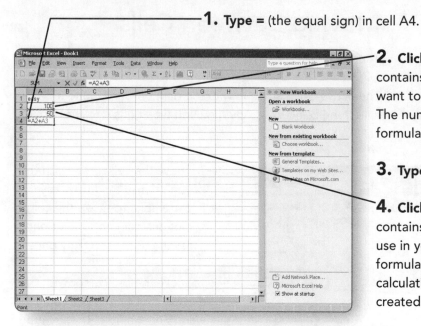

2. Click on **cell A2**, which contains the first number you want to use in the calculation. The number will be used in the formula in A4.

3. Type + (the plus sign).

4. Click on **cell A3**, which contains the second number to use in your formula. In the formula bar, you will see the calculation that has been created.

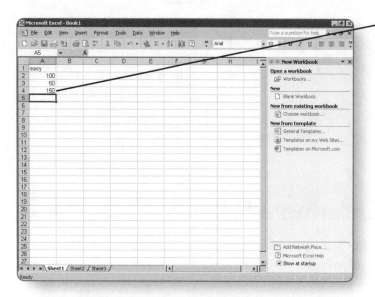

5. Press the **Enter key**. The formula will perform the calculation, and the result will appear in the active cell.

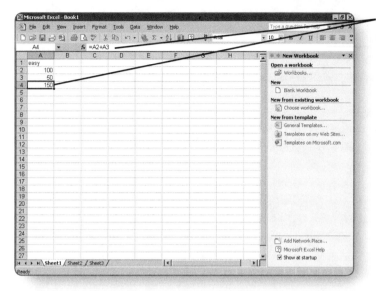

If you move the pointer back up to the cell where the answer appears, you can see that the cell contains the result, but if you look at the formula bar, you can see that it still displays the formula you created.

Playing "What If?"

The formula remains stored in the cell so that you can change either of the numbers used in the calculation at any time.

1. Click on **cell A3**. The cell will be highlighted.

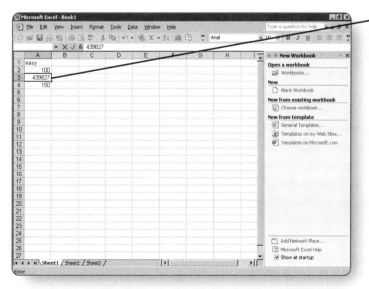

2. Type a **different number**. The number will appear in the cell.

3. Press the **Enter key**. Excel will automatically recalculate the total in A4.

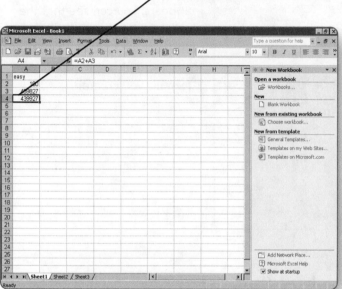

Excel can perform the calculation because it not only displays the result in the cell, but it also stores the formula. The formula isn't 100 + 50, which is how you calculate on a calculator, but A2 + A3, which still appears in the formula bar.

This is one of the main reasons why Excel is so powerful. After you've set up a relationship between cells in a formula, you can change any of the numbers in those cells, but the relationship in the formula remains. Formulas are covered in greater detail in Chapter 6.

2

What's on the Excel Screen?

A multitude of buttons and icons appears in the Excel window. Some icons make it easy to guess what the button does; however, some are less obvious. Learning to use all the elements of the Excel screen is an important part of using Excel. In this chapter, you'll learn how to:

- Select menu commands
- Use toolbars
- Work with dialog boxes
- Use the task pane
- Display or hide on-screen controls
- Get help

Using Menus

Menus are lists of commands, options, and other program features that you can activate. For example, you can choose a menu command to underline text or save your work.

1. Click on the **name of the menu** that you want to open. The menu will appear.

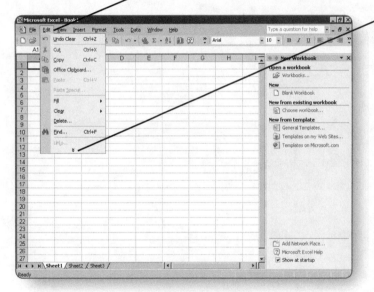

2. Pause a **moment**, or **click** the **down arrow** at the bottom of the menu. The complete list of menu items will appear.

NOTE

By default, Excel uses personalized menus. This means that not all available commands appear on the menu initially— only an abbreviated set based on past usage (or a default abbreviated set if you have not used Excel before). If you want Excel to show the complete menu immediately, see "Changing How Menus and Toolbars Work" later in this chapter.

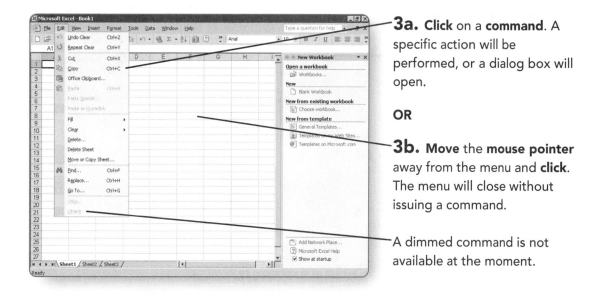

3a. **Click** on a **command**. A specific action will be performed, or a dialog box will open.

OR

3b. **Move** the **mouse pointer** away from the menu and **click**. The menu will close without issuing a command.

A dimmed command is not available at the moment.

Understanding Menu Items

Excel's menus contain various items that give you at-a-glance information about a menu's commands.

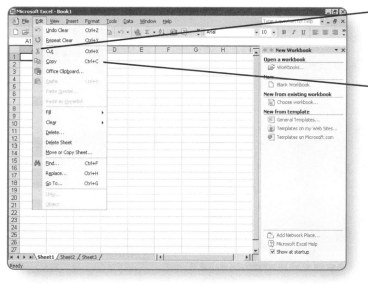

A picture indicates that there is a toolbar equivalent for the command.

Keyboard shortcuts, alternatives to using the menu command, are listed when available.

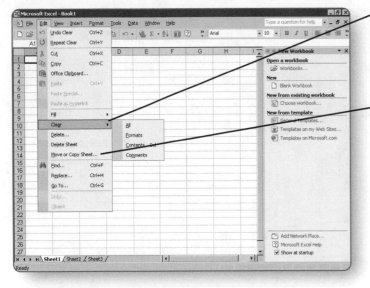

A right-pointing arrow indicates that a submenu is available. Pointing to the command opens the submenu.

An ellipsis (. . .) next to a command indicates that a dialog box will open when you click on that command. See "Working with Dialog Boxes" later in this chapter.

Using Shortcut Menus

You can right-click on almost any cell or other object in Excel to open a context-sensitive shortcut menu. The menu contains commands applicable to that object.

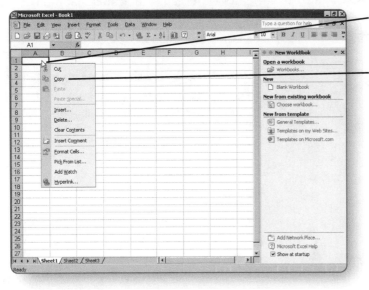

1. Right-click on a **cell**. A shortcut menu will appear.

2. Click (normally, with the left mouse button) on a **command**.

To close the menu without making a selection, click an area away from the menu.

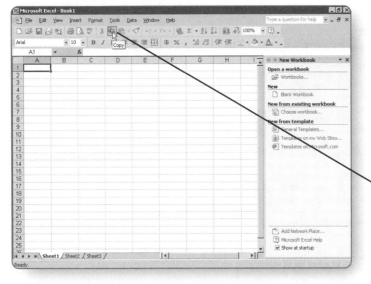

Using Toolbars

Toolbars are organized groups of buttons and other controls that issue commands or apply formatting. They serve as alternatives to using the menu commands.

1. Move the **mouse pointer** over any button in the toolbar. The button name will appear.

2. Click on a **toolbar button**. The command associated with the button will execute.

Using Lists on Toolbars

Some controls on the toolbars employ drop-down lists, which are somewhat like menus. Such controls have down-pointing arrows to their right.

1. Click on a **down arrow** next to a button or other control. A drop-down list will appear.

2. Click on your **selection** from the list.

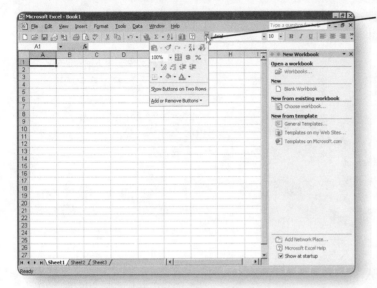

Because the Standard and Formatting toolbars share a row, some toolbar controls are not visible. To see them, click the >> button at the right end of the toolbar to open a drop-down list of additional controls.

NOTE

To place the Standard and Formatting toolbars on separate rows, so that all the tools are visible for each toolbar, see "Changing How Menus and Toolbars Work" later in this chapter.

Working with Dialog Boxes

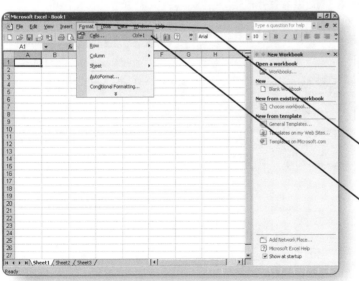

Many menu commands are followed by three dots (an ellipsis . . .). This indicates that a dialog box opens when you select the command. Here's an example.

1. Click on **Format**. The Format menu will appear.

2. Click on **Cells**. The Format Cells dialog box will open.

Notice how related options have been grouped together on tabbed panels to make things easier to find. You can select from the groups Number, Alignment, Font, Border, Patterns, and Protection.

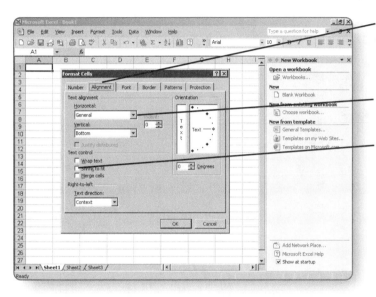

3. Click on the **Alignment tab**. The Alignment options will appear.

● Select from drop-down lists by clicking on a down arrow.

● Turn features on or off by clicking on a box to insert or remove a check mark.

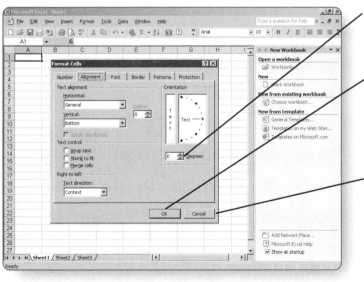

● Adjust numbers in dialog boxes by clicking on up and down arrows.

4a. Click on **OK**. Selections made in the dialog box will be implemented.

OR

4b. Click on **Cancel**. The dialog box will close, and no changes will be made.

Using the Task Pane

The task pane is a new feature common to all Office XP programs. It provides shortcuts to common commands and features. The task pane is context sensitive, which means its content changes depending on what task you are performing. You can also change it manually.

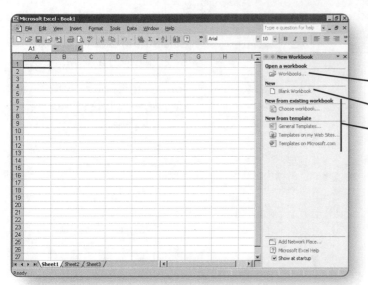

When you start Excel, the New Workbook task pane appears. You can use it to:

- Open a saved workbook
- Start a new blank workbook
- Create a new workbook based on an existing one or based on a template

Displaying Different Task Panes

At least two other task panes are available at all times: the Clipboard task pane and the Search task pane. Others might sometimes be available too, depending on what you are doing.

1. Click on the **down arrow** in the upper-right corner of the task pane. A list of available task panes will open.

2. Click on the **task pane** you want to view. The content of the task pane window will change.

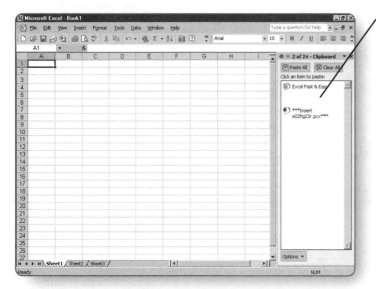

For example, here is the Clipboard task pane, which shows the content of the Office XP Clipboard. The Clipboard can hold up to 24 cut or copied pieces of data. You will learn more about it in Chapter 5.

Working with the Status Bar

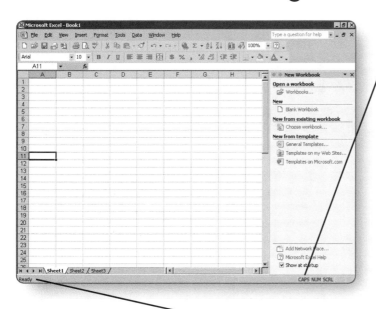

The status bar is at the bottom of the Excel window.

At the right end of the status bar is an indicator area that shows whether the CAPS lock, the NUM lock for the numeric keypad, or the SCRL lock are activated. If they are, an abbreviation appears in one of these boxes; if they aren't active, the blocks are empty. In this screen, all three locks, CAPS, NUM, and SCRL, are activated.

A status indicator appears at the far left end of the status bar. Most of the time, the status bar reads "Ready." When this setting is showing, you can work with the worksheet.

Displaying or Hiding On-Screen Controls

The task pane, toolbars, formula bar, and status bar all appear on-screen by default, but you can hide any or all of them to gain more space for your worksheet's rows and columns. Many people prefer to hide the task pane, for example, since it takes up so much space on-screen.

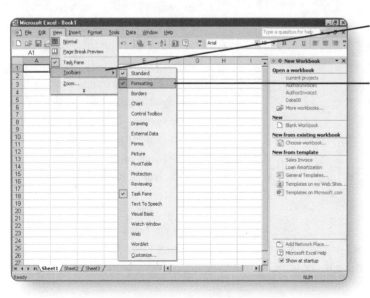

1. **Click** on **View**. The View menu will appear.

On-screen controls that are currently displayed have check marks.

2a. **Click** on **Task Pane**, **Formula Bar**, or **Status Bar** to turn that element off or on. Then skip step 3.

OR

2b. **Point** to **Toolbars**. A list of toolbars will appear.

3. **Click** on the **name of the toolbar** that you want to turn off or on.

Changing How Menus and Toolbars Work

Some people do not like Excel 2000's new menu and toolbar features. You might prefer that the menus show a full list of commands immediately or that the Standard and Formatting toolbars appear on separate rows.

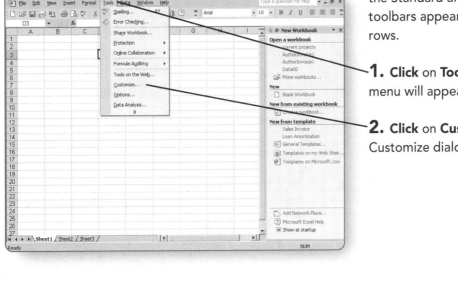

1. **Click** on **Tools**. The Tools menu will appear.

2. **Click** on **Customize**. The Customize dialog box will open.

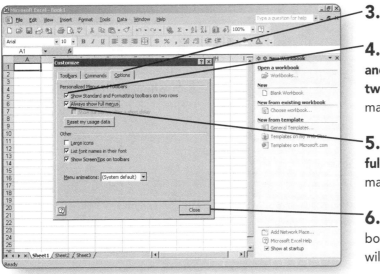

3. **Click** on the **Options tab**.

4. **Click** on the **Show Standard and Formatting toolbars on two rows check box**. A check mark will appear.

5. **Click** on the **Always show full menus check box**. A check mark will appear.

6. **Click** on **Close**. The dialog box will close, and the changes will take effect.

NOTE

In the rest of this book, the figures will show the Standard and Formatting toolbars on separate rows and the full menus rather than the personalized ones.

Moving Around the Screen with Scroll Bars

You can move around an Excel worksheet in several ways.

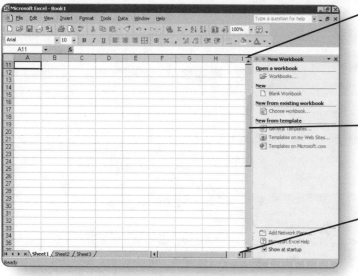

1. Click repeatedly on the **arrow** at either end of the vertical scroll bar. The worksheet will move up or down in the window.

2. Hold the **mouse button** and **drag** the **vertical scroll box** up or down. The worksheet will scroll quickly up or down.

3. Click repeatedly on the **arrow** at either end of the horizontal scroll bar. The worksheet will move left or right.

Getting Help

There are many ways to use the Help system in Excel, but the newest and most convenient is to type a question or term in the Ask a Question box.

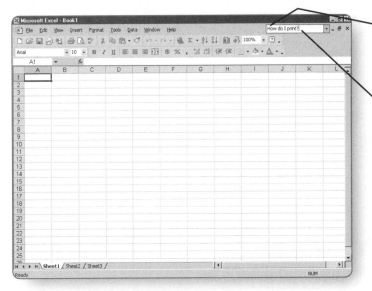

1. Click on the **Ask a Question box**. An insertion point will appear there.

2. Type your **question**, or a few words that describe what you need help with.

3. Press Enter. A menu of help topics will appear.

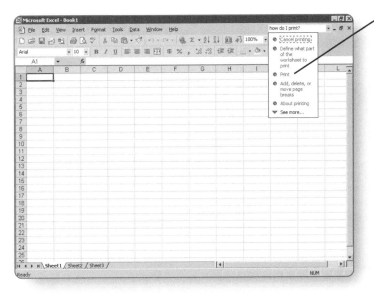

4. Click on the **topic button** representing the subject you need help with. The topic will appear in the Microsoft Excel Help window.

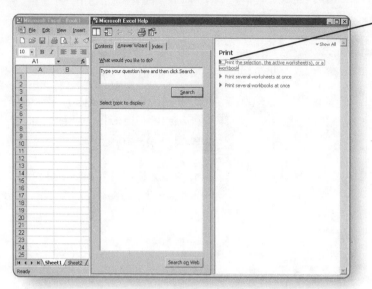

5. Click the **topic** you want to read about. Text below the topic will expand.

6. Read the **Help information** that appears.

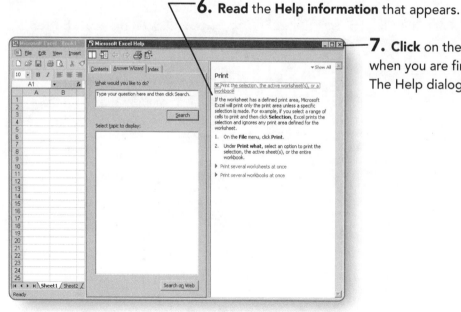

7. Click on the **Close button** when you are finished with Help. The Help dialog box will close.

3

Saving, Printing, and Exiting Excel

Everyone who uses a computer has probably lost data at one time or another. If you haven't been saving to a disk regularly, remember that it only takes a few seconds to lose hours of work. You'll also probably want to make printouts of your work to share with others. You could use the hard copy as a report or possibly on a transparency as part of a presentation. In this chapter, you'll learn how to:

- Save a worksheet
- Print your work
- Close a workbook
- Exit Excel

Saving Your Work

Computer users know they must save their work, but many forget, until something important is lost. Not only is it important to save your work so that you don't have to redo it, but saving also gives you the opportunity to file your work electronically, so that you know where to find it.

1. Click on the **Save button**. If this is the first time you've saved the document, the Save As dialog box will open.

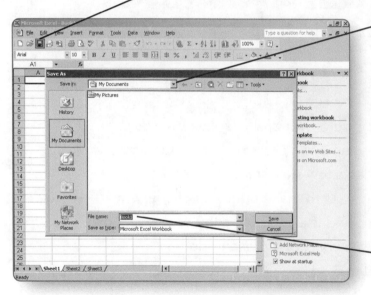

The Save in drop-down list offers you a folder where you can save your worksheet. If you haven't made any changes to your software, the default folder that appears is the My Documents folder. If you want to select a different disk or folder, click on the down arrow.

CAUTION

Excel will offer you "Book1" as a name. It's not a good idea to accept this because by the time you get to "Book9," it's going to be difficult to remember what exactly you saved in Book3 or Book4.

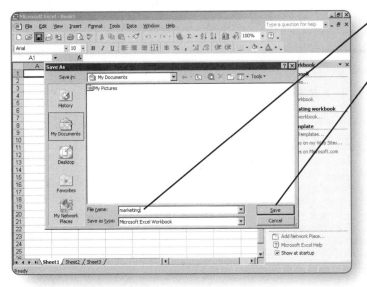

2. **Type** a **name** for your file in the File name text box.

3. **Click** on **Save**. Your document will be stored on a disk.

Excel automatically adds an .xls extension to the file name. This indicates the file format used to save Excel files.

4. **Click** on the **Save button** regularly to continue to save your document as you work on it. The Save As dialog box will not open again.

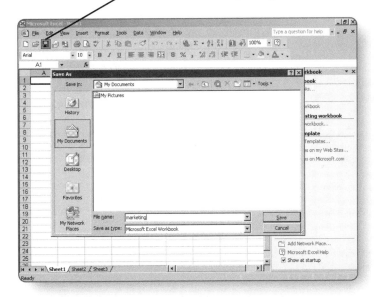

TIP

If you want to save a copy of your file with a different name, click on File and Save As to open the Save As dialog box again.

Changing the Save Location

The default save location of C:\My Documents is adequate for most people. However, you might sometimes want to save somewhere else, such as to a floppy disk or a backup folder.

1. Click on the **down arrow** next to Save in. A list of drives and other locations will appear.

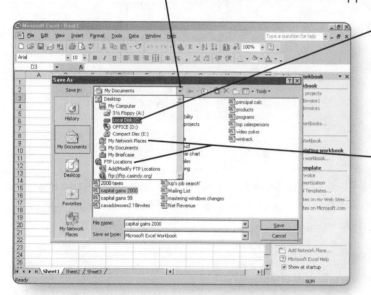

2. Click on the **drive** on which you want to save. A list of the folders on that drive will appear, if there are any.

NOTE

Some of the non-drive items on the menu include My Network Places (for network saves) and FTP Locations (for Internet saves). These steps focus on saving to a drive, but you might want to experiment with other locations on your own.

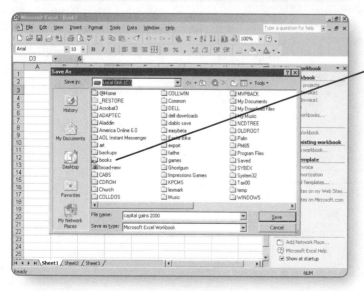

3. Double-click on the **folder** in which to save. The folder's name will appear in the Save in box.

4. Repeat step 3 to move to deeper levels of subfolders if needed to locate the folder you want.

5. Continue saving normally.

Printing a Worksheet

Whether you need to share a budget report with your colleagues or your retirement savings projection with your spouse, you need to print your file on paper.

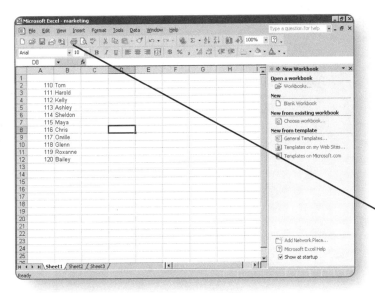

Printing with the Print Button

If you just need one copy of the worksheet you currently are working on, the fastest and easiest way to print is to use the Print button on the Standard toolbar.

1. **Click** on the **Print button**. One copy of everything on the current worksheet will be immediately sent to the printer.

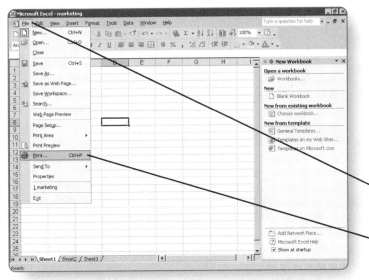

Printing with the Print Dialog Box

If you need to print multiple copies, or a specific range of cells, or you need to change which printer is being used, you must open the Print dialog box.

1. **Click** on **File**. The File menu will appear.

2. **Click** on **Print**. The Print dialog box will open.

3. Set any of the **following options**:

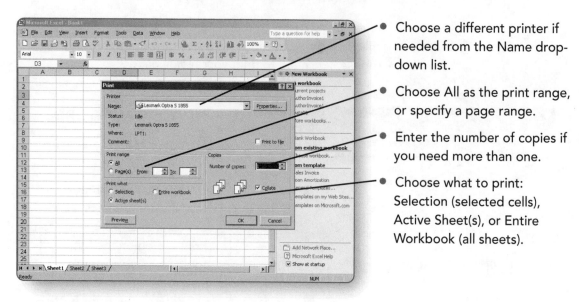

- Choose a different printer if needed from the Name drop-down list.

- Choose All as the print range, or specify a page range.

- Enter the number of copies if you need more than one.

- Choose what to print: Selection (selected cells), Active Sheet(s), or Entire Workbook (all sheets).

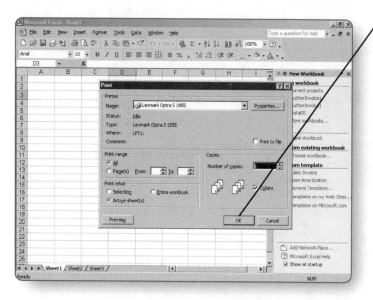

4. Click on **OK** when you've made your selections. The pages will be sent to the printer.

NOTE

If you do not want the entire worksheet or workbook printed, select the range of cells you want to print before performing these steps. See Chapter 5, "Editing Worksheets," to learn about selecting cells.

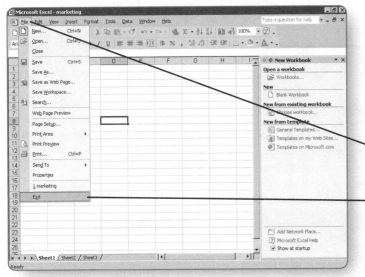

Exiting Excel

You can exit Excel in several ways. This section shows you how to exit by using the menu bar.

1. Click on **File**. The File menu will appear.

2. Click on **Exit**. The Excel program will close.

If an open workbook hasn't been saved, a dialog box asks whether you want to save changes to that particular file.

- Click on Yes to save the workbook specified and exit. If you haven't previously saved the workbook, the Save As dialog box will open.

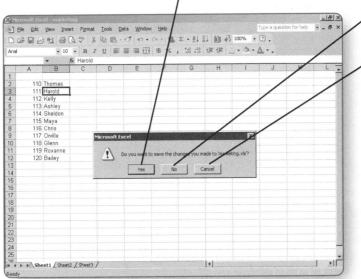

- Click on No to exit Excel without saving any changes.

- Click on Cancel to return to the Excel program without closing any workbooks.

NOTE

If you have more than one workbook open with unsaved changes, the message also includes a Yes to All option. Choosing this is the same as choosing Yes for each workbook individually.

4

Managing Workbooks and Worksheets

A *workbook* is an electronic file that contains one or more worksheets. The *worksheets* are like pages of a book that are available to you when your book (workbook) is open. Just as you can have different folders or books piled on the top of your desk at one time, you can have more than one workbook open at a time in Excel. You can easily switch between workbooks and worksheets as well. In this chapter, you'll learn how to:

- Create a new workbook
- Move between workbooks
- View multiple workbooks
- Open and close workbooks
- Add, name, and delete worksheets

Creating a New Workbook

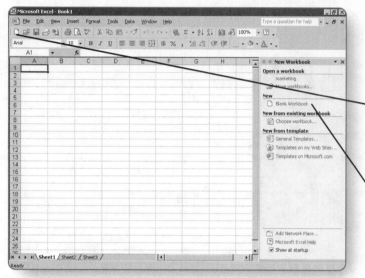

Before you can learn to manage workbooks and worksheets, you must know how to create a new workbook.

1a. **Click** on the **New button** on the toolbar.

OR

1b. **Click** on **Blank Workbook** on the task pane. A new workbook will open.

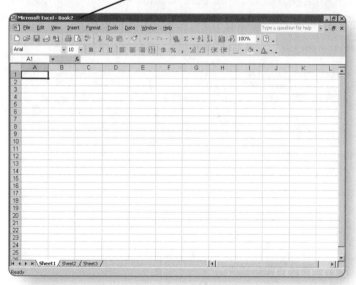

The name shown for the new workbook reflects how many workbooks you've created during this session. The workbook that opens automatically when you start Excel is Book1; the next one is Book2; and so on.

TIP

When you start a new workbook, the task pane disappears, but you can get it back at any time by opening the View menu and clicking on Task Pane.

Moving Between Workbooks

Often your work requires you to work with multiple workbooks. Excel enables you to move easily between more than one workbook.

1. **Click** on **Window**. The Window menu will appear.

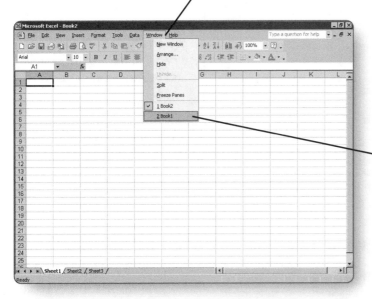

At the bottom of the Window menu is a list of the files you have open. The file with the check mark next to it is the file that you are currently working on in the main Excel window.

2. **Click** on the **file name** of the file you want to work with. The file you specify will be displayed on-screen.

Viewing Multiple Workbooks

In Excel, you can have more than one workbook open and view more than one workbook on-screen at a time. You can also view workbooks tiled on the screen with the screen divided into multiple windows, one for each workbook.

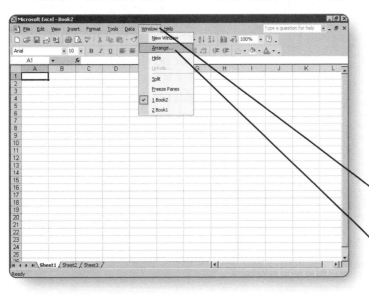

1. **Click** on **Window**. The Window menu will appear.

2. **Click** on **Arrange**. The Arrange Windows dialog box will open.

3. **Click** on **Tiled**. The item will be selected.

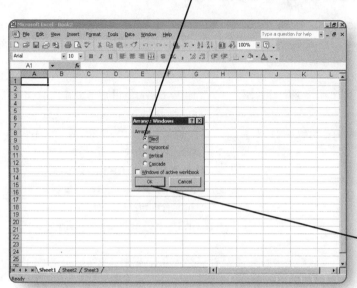

NOTE

For this exercise you're choosing Tiled, but you can choose one of the other arrangement options instead if you prefer. Try each of them when you have extra time and observe their effects.

4. **Click** on **OK**. The workbooks will be tiled on-screen.

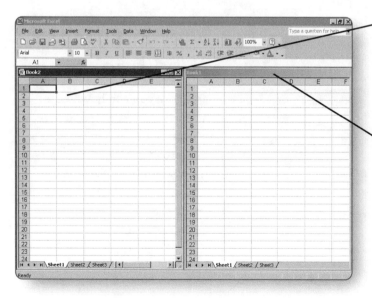

You can work in any of the workbooks by clicking in it to make it active. Use the scroll bar to move quickly through the worksheet data.

To maximize one workbook, so that it fills the entire work area, click twice (double-click) on the title bar for that workbook.

Closing a Workbook

Closing a workbook gets it out of the way, reducing screen clutter. It also frees up the memory that the computer was using to display it. You might close a workbook when you are finished with it but are not yet finished working in Excel. (If you were finished with both that workbook and Excel in general, you could simply exit Excel and the workbook will close automatically.)

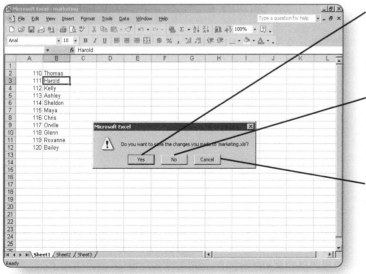

1. **Click** on **File**. The File menu will appear.

2. **Click** on **Close**. If you have made any changes to the workbook since you last saved it, a dialog box will appear and ask whether you want to save changes.

3a. **Click** on **Yes** to save changes.

OR

3b. **Click** on **No** to close the workbook without saving.

OR

3c. **Click** on **Cancel** to go back to the workbook.

Opening an Existing Workbook

You can open an existing workbook (a workbook that has previously been saved on a disk) in two ways. If you've been working on the workbook recently, it probably will still be listed at the bottom of the File menu. If it's not listed, you'll need to search for its location on a disk.

Opening a Recently Used File

Excel keeps the last four files you have worked with handy, by listing them at the bottom of the File menu and also under the Open a workbook heading on the task pane.

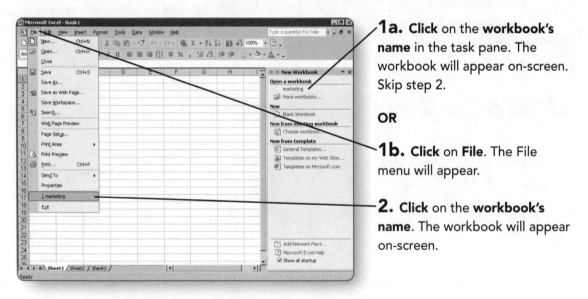

1a. Click on the **workbook's name** in the task pane. The workbook will appear on-screen. Skip step 2.

OR

1b. Click on **File**. The File menu will appear.

2. Click on the **workbook's name**. The workbook will appear on-screen.

Opening a File with the Open Dialog Box

If you want to open a file that is not one of the four most recently used, you must access the Open dialog box. There are several ways to do so.

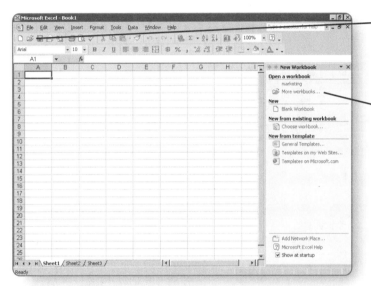

1a. **Click** the **Open button** on the toolbar.

OR

1b. **Click** on **More workbooks** in the task pane. The Open dialog box will open.

TIP

Yet another variation on step 1 is to open the File menu and click on the Open command.

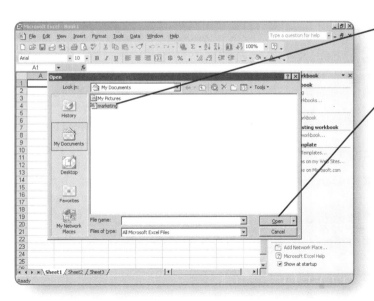

2. **Click** on the **file** you want to open. The file will be highlighted.

3. **Click** on **Open**. The selected file will appear on-screen.

NOTE

If the file you want is not in the default folder (C:\My Documents), see the procedure described next.

Opening a File from Another Location

If the file you want does not appear on the list of files shown by default in the Open dialog box, you must change the drive and/or folder that this dialog box shows. This is very similar to the procedure in Chapter 3 for saving to a different location.

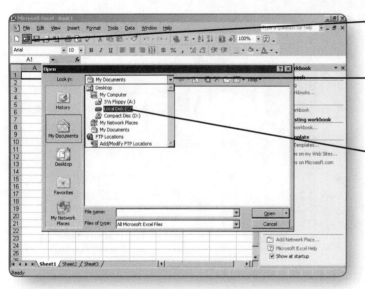

1. **Click** on the **Open button**. The Open dialog box will open.

2. **Click** the **down arrow** next to the Look in box. The drop-down list will appear.

3. **Click** on the **drive** that contains the file. The drive's contents will appear.

Some drives contain multiple folders. If the file is stored in a folder, you will need to navigate into that folder. If the drive does not contain folders (a floppy disk might not, for example), you can skip step 4.

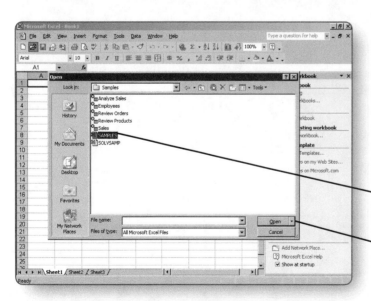

4. If needed, **double-click** on the **folder** to move to. You may have to navigate through several layers of folders to find the file. The folder name will appear in the Look in box.

5. **Click** on the **file** you want to open. The file will be selected.

6. **Click** on **Open**. The file will open.

Working with Worksheets

By default, each new workbook has three worksheets. A Sheet tab appears for each worksheet at the bottom of the workbook window.

1. Click on a **worksheet tab** to move to a different worksheet. The new worksheet will appear on-screen.

Naming a Worksheet

To organize and effectively manage your worksheets, give your worksheets names that remind you of what information they contain.

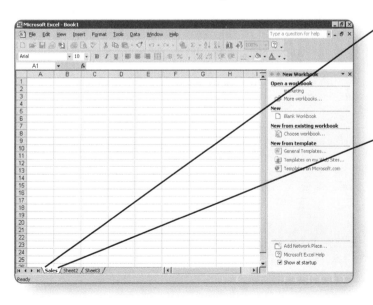

1. Double-click on the **tab** for the sheet you want to name. The current name will be highlighted and ready for editing.

2. Type a **new name**.

3. Click anywhere **outside the tab**. The name change will appear on the tab you selected.

Adding Worksheets to a Workbook

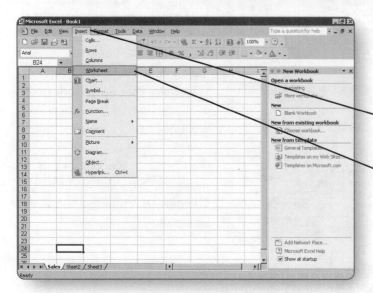

Excel gives you three worksheets for every workbook, but adding more worksheets is not a problem.

1. **Click** on **Insert**. The Insert menu will appear.

2. **Click** on **Worksheet**. A new worksheet will be added to your workbook.

NOTE

All the worksheets are saved each time you save the workbook.

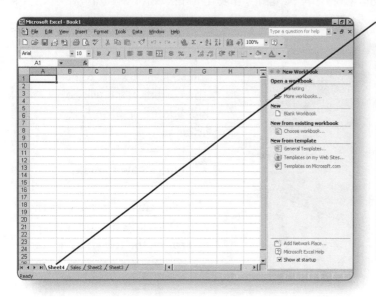

Notice that the new worksheet is added to the left of the worksheet that was active (on top) when you issued the command.

NOTE

You can rearrange the order of the tabs on the screen by clicking on one of the tabs and dragging it to a new location.

Deleting a Worksheet

If you no longer need a worksheet, it's easy to get rid of it.

1. Click on **Edit**. The Edit menu will appear.

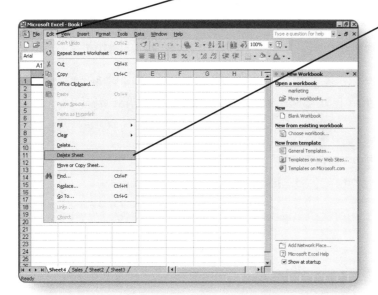

2. Click on **Delete Sheet**. A dialog box will open and tell you that the sheet will be permanently deleted.

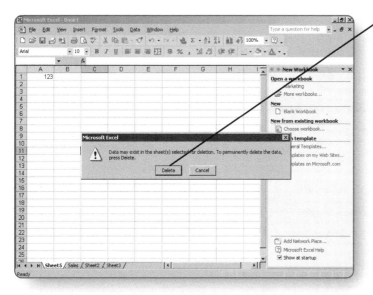

3. Click on **Delete**. The worksheet will be deleted.

Part I Review Questions

1. What does a designation like B5 mean? *See "Entering Text and Numbers" in Chapter 1*

2. What are labels? *See "Entering Text and Numbers" in Chapter 1*

3. What happens to a cell that contains a formula when you change the number in a cell that it references? *See "Playing 'What If?'" in Chapter 1*

4. What does it mean when an ellipsis (. . .) appears after a menu command? *See "Understanding Menu Items" in Chapter 2*

5. How do you display a shortcut menu? *See "Using Shortcut Menus" in Chapter 2*

6. How can you save a copy of a file under a different name? *See "Saving Your Work" in Chapter 3*

7. What happens when you click on the Print button? *See "Printing with the Print Button" in Chapter 3*

8. What is the difference between a workbook and a worksheet? *See the introduction of Chapter 4*

9. How can you switch between workbooks when you have more than one workbook open? *See "Moving Between Workbooks" in Chapter 4*

10. When you insert a new worksheet into a workbook, where does Excel place the new worksheet? *See "Adding Worksheets to a Workbook" in Chapter 4*

PART II

Constructing Larger Worksheets

5

Editing Worksheets

When you create a worksheet, a lot of data entry is involved. Excel has features to cut down on at least some of that repetitive work. Unfortunately, you'll still make mistakes, so you need to know how to edit cell entries and run the spelling checker. You'll probably also want to make some changes to the way you construct your worksheet. Some great features in Excel allow you to reorganize your worksheet without having to reenter any data. In this chapter, you'll learn how to:

- Select and edit cells
- Add and delete data, rows, and columns
- Copy and move data
- Fill and transpose ranges
- Adjust column width and row height
- Check spelling in a worksheet

Selecting Cells

Before you can work with many of the features in Excel, you need to know how to select cells. You can select a rectangular group of cells, called a *range*, in any of the following ways:

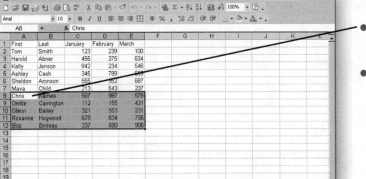

- Click and drag over the selection.

- Click in one cell, and then hold down the Shift key and click in the opposite corner of the selection.

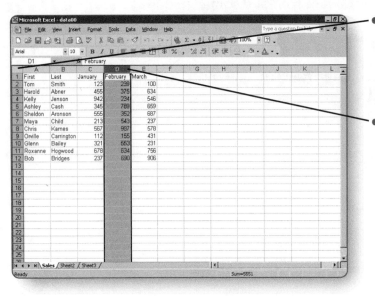

- Click on the Select All button, the gray rectangle where the column and row headings meet, to select the entire worksheet.

- Click in a column or row heading to select the whole column or row.

Editing Cell Content

When a cell is selected, its content appears in the formula bar. You can edit the content by clicking to place the insertion point there and then using standard text editing keys. For example, you can delete characters using the Backspace key. You can also move the insertion point with the arrow keys and either insert text by typing or delete text by pressing the Delete or Backspace keys.

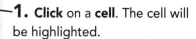

1. Click on a **cell**. The cell will be highlighted.

2. Click in the **formula bar** to place the insertion point in the entry. You will now be able to insert or delete text.

3. Press the **right** or **left arrow key** to move the insertion point where you need to make a change.

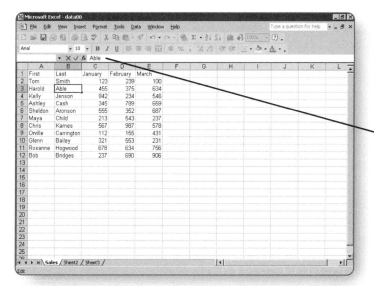

4. Press the **Backspace key** to delete the character to the left of the insertion point, or **press** the **Delete key** to delete the character to the right.

5. Type new text as needed. The text will appear in the formula bar and the selected cell.

6. Press the **Enter key**. The change will be accepted.

Replacing Cell Content

You can completely replace the content of a cell, rather than edit it.

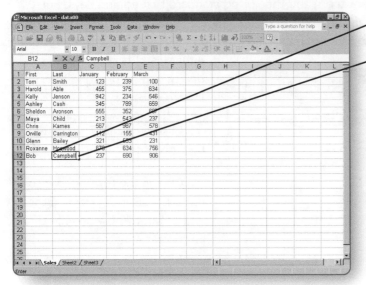

1. Click on a **cell**.

2. Type the **new content**. Whatever you type will replace the old content.

3. Press the **Enter key**. The change will be accepted.

Removing Cell Content

You can remove all content from a single cell or a range of cells, leaving the cell or cells blank.

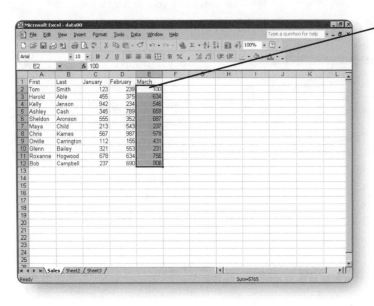

1. Select the **cell** or **range of cells** to clear.

2. Press the **Delete key**. The cells will be cleared.

NOTE

This procedure clears the content from the cell but leaves the empty cell in place. To remove the cell, so that surrounding content shifts, use the Delete command on the Edit menu.

Adding Rows and Columns

As you construct your worksheet, you'll occasionally find that you need to add rows and columns. To add a new row, you first select the row that the new one should appear above. Or, to add a new column, you select the column that the new one should appear to the left of.

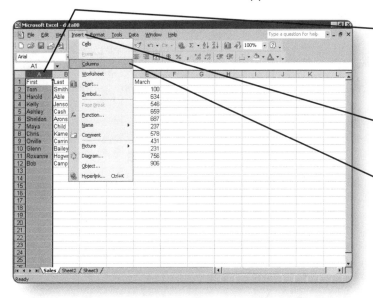

1. Click in a **row** or **column head** to select it. The row or column you choose will be highlighted.

2. Click on **Insert**. The Insert menu will appear.

3. Click on **Rows** or **Columns**. The new row or column will be inserted before the row or column you initially selected.

NOTE

Depending on whether you select a row or column, the menu item for a row or column will be either available or dimmed.

Notice that the old column A becomes column B and the remaining columns also move over one column to the right, and a new column A is displayed.

Oops!—Using Undo and Redo

Sometimes you'll want to undo an action you've just completed in Excel.

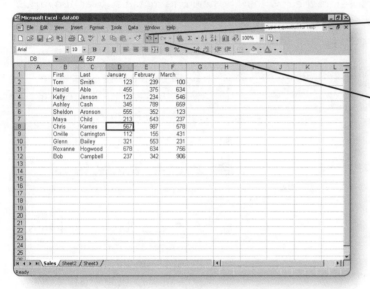

1. Click on the **Undo button**. The last action you performed will be undone.

If you make a mistake by undoing, immediately click the Redo button to get back what was undone.

Undoing Multiple Actions

After working in a worksheet for a while, there will be many levels of Undo that you can work back through.

1. Click on the **down arrow** next to the Undo button. Your recent actions will be listed.

2. Click on the **action** you want to undo. That action and all actions you took after it will be undone.

> ### NOTE
>
> The Redo button also has a drop-down list, for multiple-action redoing.

Moving Data

One advantage of using Excel is the ease with which you can move and copy data.

1. **Select** a **range of cells**. The cells will be highlighted.

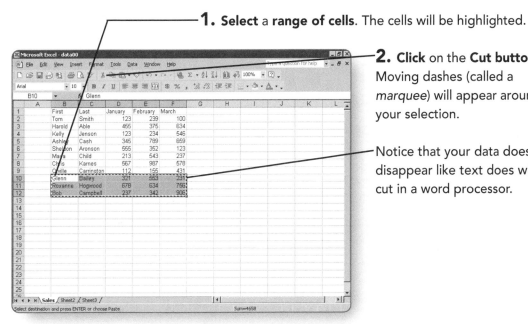

2. **Click** on the **Cut button**. Moving dashes (called a *marquee*) will appear around your selection.

Notice that your data doesn't disappear like text does when cut in a word processor.

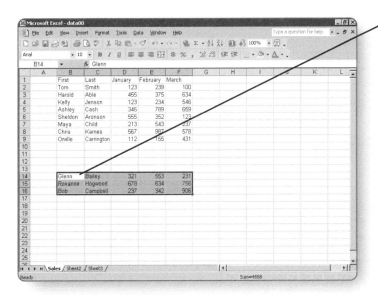

3. **Click** in the **cell** that will be the upper-left corner of the new location of the range. The cell will be selected.

> ### NOTE
> There must be enough empty cells in the new location to accommodate the cut data or existing data will be overwritten.

4. Click on the **Paste button**. The data will be pasted in the new location.

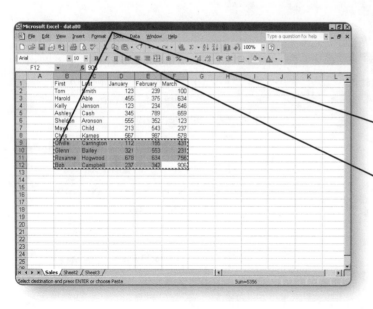

NOTE

Here's a quirk that's unique to Excel: the Cut command does not place the data on the Clipboard. Only the Copy command places Excel data on the Clipboard. When you use Cut and Paste to move a selection, Excel stores the selection in memory, but you cannot reuse it from the Clipboard after pasting.

Copying Data

Copying places selected data in a new location. Unlike moved data, copied data also remains in the original location.

1. Select a **range of cells**. The cells will be highlighted.

2. Click on the **Copy button**. A marquee will appear around your selection.

3. Click in the **cell** at the upper-left corner of the range where you want to place the copy.

4. Click on the **Paste button**. The selected range will appear in both the original location and the new location.

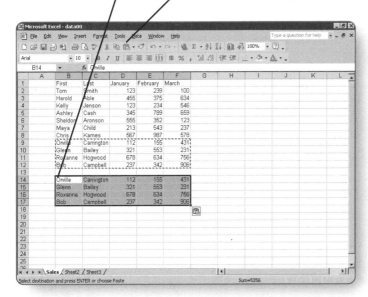

5. (Optional) **Repeat steps 3 and 4**. Another copy of the same selection will be pasted in a different spot.

6. Press the **Esc key** to turn off the marquee around the selection.

TIP

You can also use shortcut keys as a substitute for the Cut, Copy, and Paste buttons. To cut, press Ctrl+X; to copy, press Ctrl+C; and to paste, press Ctrl+V. Many experienced Excel users find these keyboard shortcuts more expedient than the toolbar buttons because they do not have to take their hand away from the keyboard to move the mouse.

Using Clipboard Copy Options

Office XP programs, including Excel, come with an enhanced Clipboard that offers extra pasting features compared to other Windows-based programs.

Specifying Paste Options

When you paste a copied selection from the Clipboard, a Paste icon appears in the lower-right corner of the selection. You can click this icon to open a menu of Paste options that control how the pasted selection appears:

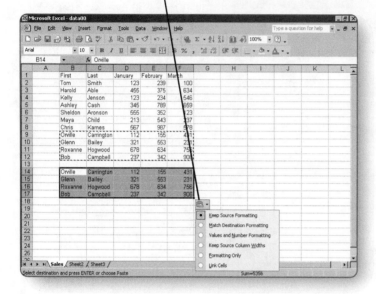

- **Keep Source Formatting**. Copies the formatting as well as the data from the original.

- **Match Destination Formatting**. Applies whatever formatting is already in the destination cells, if any.

- **Values and Number Formatting**. If the original contained formulas, copies only the results of those formulas and applies number formatting.

- **Keep Source Column Widths**. Resizes the columns to match the widths of the original selection.

- **Formatting Only**. Copies only the cell formatting, not the data.

- **Link Cells**. Creates references to each of the copied cells rather than copying the values. For example, copying the content of D1 to D15 would place the formula =D1 in cell D15.

Until you click away from the selection, completing the Paste operation, you can reopen this menu and change your selection as many times as you wish.

Using the Clipboard Task Pane

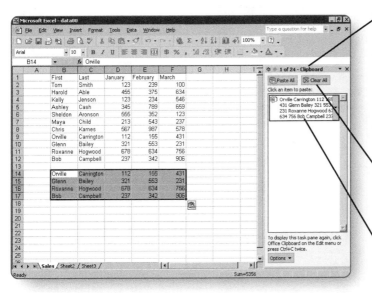

The Clipboard task pane appears when you use Copy twice before using Paste. You can also manually display the Clipboard task pane, as you learned in "Displaying Different Task Panes" in Chapter 2.

Click Clear All to clear the Clipboard task pane of all selections.

The Clipboard holds up to 24 separate copied selections. To paste one other than the most recently copied, click the selection to paste.

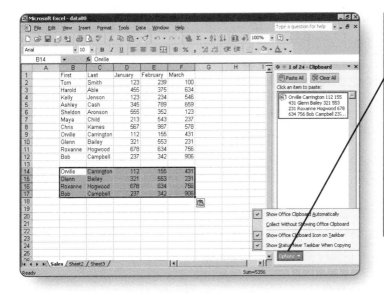

NOTE

Click the Options button in the Clipboard task pane to control whether the Clipboard appears automatically, whether its icon appears on the Taskbar when it's open, and whether to show the Clipboard status near the Taskbar when copying.

Using Drag and Drop

A quick way to move or copy, if you're good with a mouse, is by using the Drag-and-Drop feature. Drag-and-Drop bypasses the Clipboard entirely.

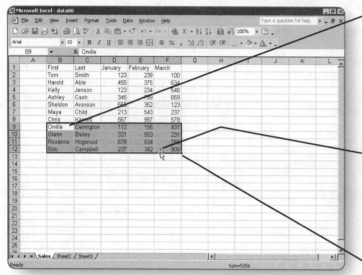

1. Select the **cells** you want to move or copy. The cells will be highlighted.

2. Hold down the **Ctrl key** if you want to copy. (To move, skip this step.)

3. Position the **mouse pointer** over the border of the selected area. The mouse pointer will become an arrow with a four-headed black arrow behind it.

Avoid the lower-right corner of the range's border; this is the Fill handle and is used for a different purpose. See the next section in this chapter, "Filling a Range."

4. Press and **hold** the **mouse button** as you drag the cells to a new location. The cell location you're dragging over will appear in a box below the mouse pointer.

5. Release the **mouse button**. The cells will be dropped in the new location. This is much quicker than using buttons or menus!

Filling a Range

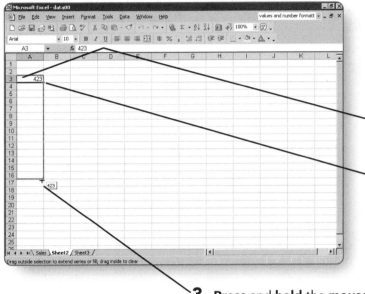

The Fill feature is for those who hate data entry. Excel can't do all the data entry for you, but it can do some of those repetitive tasks.

1. Select a **cell**. The cell will be highlighted.

2. Click on the **Fill handle** (the extra little square on the lower-right corner of the highlighted cell). The mouse pointer will change to a plus sign.

3. Press and **hold** the **mouse button** and **drag** the **Fill handle** to the right or down a number of cells.

4. Release the **mouse button**. The original contents of the highlighted cell, whether it was a number or a formula, will be copied to all the cells you selected.

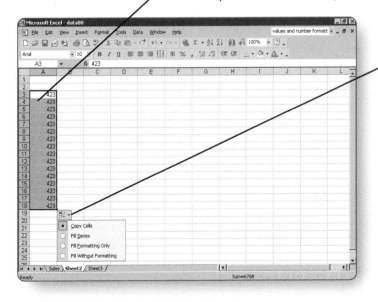

NOTE

New in Excel XP, a Fill icon appears in the lower-right corner of the filled range. You can click this icon to display a menu of Fill options. The default is to copy cells, which is what you just did. Filling with a series increments the value in each cell as it fills, as explained next.

Filling with a Series

Not only can you fill a range with a number or formula, but you also can do it with a series. This is really how the Fill feature saves you time and effort. Suppose that you need to type the months of the year to construct a budget.

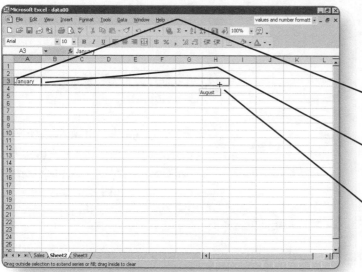

1. **Type** the **name** of a month in a cell.

2. **Click** on the **Fill handle** of that cell.

3. **Press** and **hold** the **mouse button** and **drag** the **Fill handle** to the right.

4. **Release** the **mouse button**. The months of the year following the one you typed in will be automatically inserted.

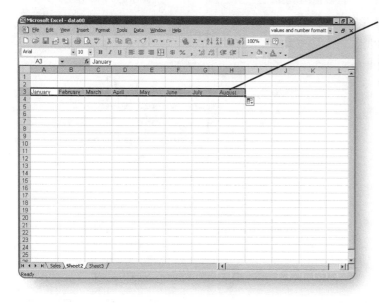

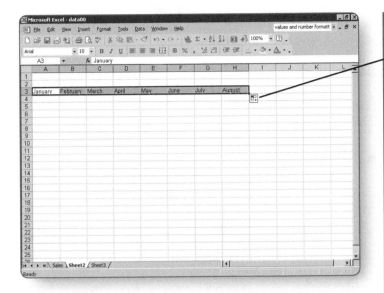

NOTE

When you start with a month name or week name, Excel assumes that you want a series (Fill Series), not the same value in each cell. In contrast, when you start with a single number, Excel assumes you want the same value (Copy Cells). You can click the Fill icon in the corner of any filled range to open a menu from which you can change the setting for the range if needed.

Transposing Cells

Imagine that you've entered five columns of data. Your fingers are aching from all that data entry, but now you realize that you don't really want the labels in a row across the top of the worksheet. The worksheet would be much more effective and easier to work with if the labels were in a column. In this situation, you use the Transpose feature. The Transpose feature switches rows of cells to columns or columns to rows.

1. Select the **cells** you want to transpose. The cells will be highlighted.

2. Click on the **Copy button**. The cells you selected will be copied to the Clipboard.

3. Click in the **cell** that will be the upper-left corner of your new range. The cell will be highlighted.

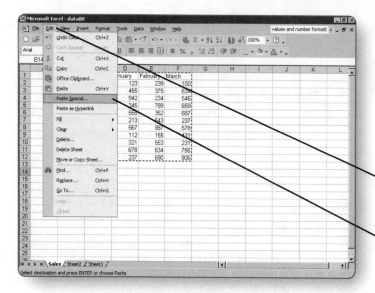

CAUTION

You can't transpose into the same range as the original location; you must choose a different location.

4. Click on **Edit**. The Edit menu will appear.

5. Click on **Paste Special**. The Paste Special dialog box will open.

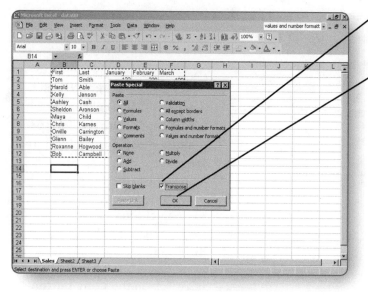

6. Click on **Transpose**. A check mark will appear in the box.

7. Click on **OK**. The dialog box will close.

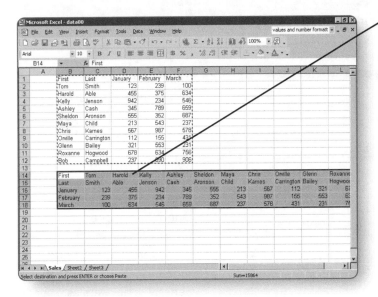

The entire table is displayed in the new location with rows converted to columns, and columns to rows.

8. Press the **Esc key**. The marquee around the original selection will be turned off.

Adjusting Column Width and Row Height

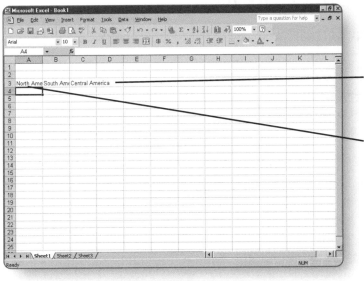

When cell content is too long to fit in its cell, one of several things may happen:

- Text labels that do not fit will spill into the next cell to the right if it is empty.

- If the next cell is not empty, text appears truncated.

● If a number is a few characters too long to fit, Excel automatically widens the cell.

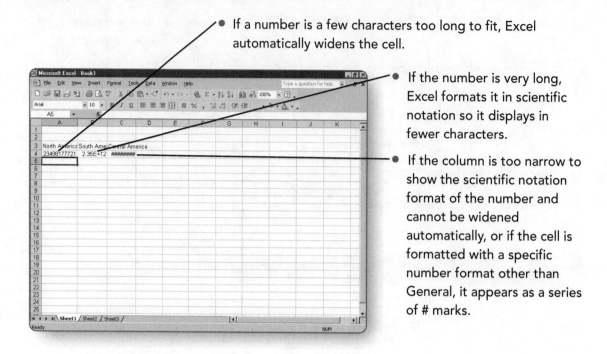

● If the number is very long, Excel formats it in scientific notation so it displays in fewer characters.

● If the column is too narrow to show the scientific notation format of the number and cannot be widened automatically, or if the cell is formatted with a specific number format other than General, it appears as a series of # marks.

Resizing a Column to Fit

You can resize a column to fit its longest entry.

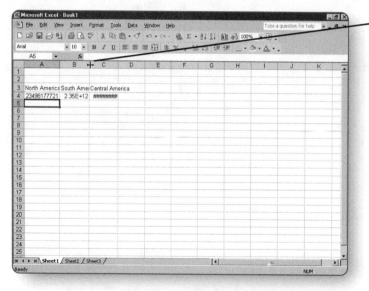

1. Double-click on the **dividing line** to the right of the column's letter. The column will automatically expand to fit the content.

Setting a Specific Column Width

You can manually widen a column (or make it more narrow) by dragging the same divider line that you double-clicked on in the preceding procedure.

1. **Move** the **mouse pointer** to the divider between the column headings on the right side of the column you want to adjust. The mouse pointer will become a double-headed arrow.

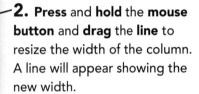

2. **Press** and **hold** the **mouse button** and **drag** the **line** to resize the width of the column. A line will appear showing the new width.

3. **Release** the **mouse button**. The changes will take effect.

There are other ways to change column width. Some are found on the Format, Column menu.

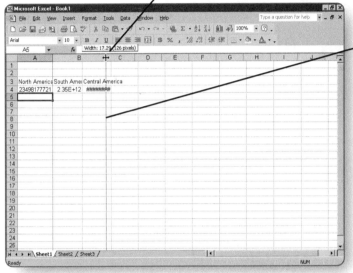

Use the Width command to open a dialog box in which you can enter a specific width, measured in characters of the default font (usually Arial 10-point).

AutoFit Selection is the same as double-clicking between the columns, except that it can apply to more than one column at a time if you select multiple columns first.

Standard Width changes the default width for columns on the worksheet.

Checking Your Spelling

After you've entered all your data, you will probably want to print your worksheet to share it with others. Before you take that step, it's a good idea to check your spelling. Even if you always won the spelling bee at school, you probably make the occasional typing error, and the Spelling feature may catch it.

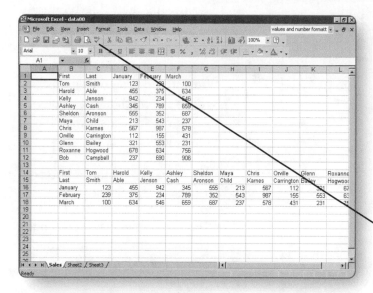

However, be aware that the Spelling feature doesn't catch all mistakes. If you've made a typing or spelling error, such as using "led" instead of "lead," because both words are in the dictionary, Spelling will not catch this as an error. Therefore, it is still very important to proofread your work.

1. Click on the **Spelling button**. The Spelling dialog box will open.

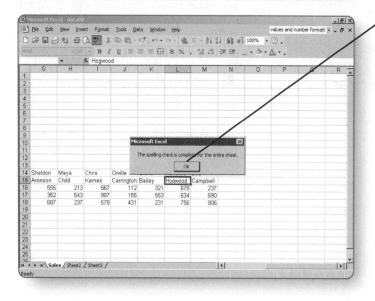

If Excel doesn't find any errors, a dialog box will open that tells you the spelling checker is complete. Click on OK, and you're done. Otherwise, continue to step 2.

NOTE

The spelling checker searches from the active cell to the end of the worksheet. If the active cell was not A1 when you began the spelling checker, then at some point during the spelling check you will see a dialog box asking whether you want to continue checking at the beginning of the sheet. Click on Yes.

At the top of the dialog box next to Not in Dictionary, Excel identifies the first item it can't match. Suggestions are listed in the Suggestions box.

2. Choose from the **following options**:

- **Ignore Once**. If the word highlighted is spelled correctly but is flagged because it does not appear in the dictionary (which often happens with proper names), click on this option to move to the next misspelling without making any changes.

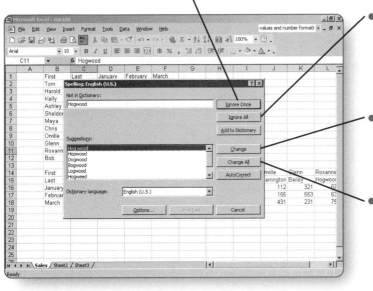

- **Ignore All**. If the highlighted word is likely to continue to occur and is spelled correctly, click on this option to ignore all future occurrences.

- **Change**. This option will change the misspelled word to the selected word in the Suggestions box.

- **Change All**. This option will change this occurrence and all subsequent occurrences of the highlighted word to the selected word in the Suggestions box.

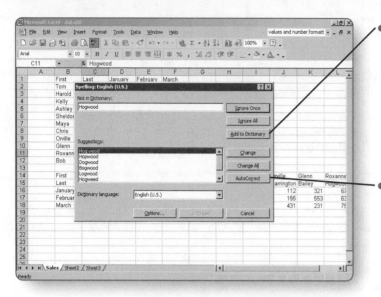

- **Add to Dictionary**. If the word is spelled correctly and you do not want Excel to continue to identify this word as a misspelling every time you run the spelling checker, click on this option to add the word to the dictionary.

- **AutoCorrect**. If a word you often misspell or mistype is identified, choose the correct spelling in the Suggestions box. You can now add the misspelled word to the list of automatic corrections by clicking on AutoCorrect. Now as you enter the word in your worksheet, it will be automatically corrected if you type or spell it incorrectly.

After Spelling is finished, a dialog box will appear telling you that the spelling checker is complete for the entire sheet.

3. Click on **OK**. The dialog box will close.

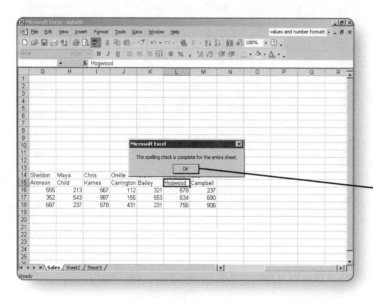

6

Using Formulas and Functions

Merely entering large quantities of data into a worksheet isn't going to help you a great deal. You need to perform calculations on that data to summarize it in a useful way. For example, you might find it helpful to know how much you really spent this year on your car or phone bill. You can then apply the information to plan, budget, find trends, or make predictions. In this chapter, you'll learn how to:

- Use the Formula palette and functions to perform calculations
- Copy formulas with relative and absolute cell references
- Use AutoCalculate
- Correct errors in formulas

Entering a Simple Calculation

To add, subtract, multiply, or divide numbers, you can use formulas. Formulas use cell references combined with the addition (+), subtraction (-), multiplication (*), and division (/) operators to perform calculations.

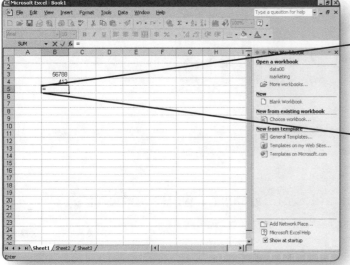

1. Click in the **cell** where you want the calculation result to appear. The cell will be highlighted.

2. Type = (equal sign). Every formula must start with one.

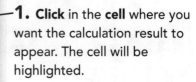

3. Click on the **cell** with the first number you want to use. Excel will enter the cell address in the selected cell and in the formula bar.

4. Type an **operator**. The operator you type will appear in the selected cell and in the formula bar.

5. Click on the **cell** with the next value you want to use in your calculation. Excel will enter the cell address in the selected cell and in the formula bar.

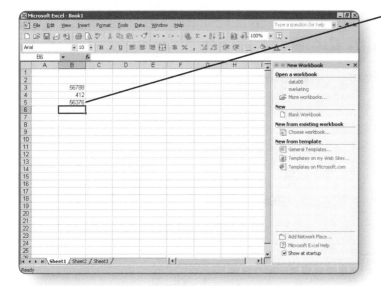

6. Press the **Enter key**. The result will be displayed in the selected cell.

NOTE

If a formula includes more than one operator, Excel calculates multiplication and division first, followed by addition and subtraction. However, you can use parentheses to control the order of precedence. Therefore, if you enter 1+2*3 the answer is 7, whereas if you enter (1+2)*3 the answer is 9.

Using Built-In Functions

Many calculations have been predefined in Excel. These built-in calculations are called *functions*. The easiest way to include a function in your worksheet is by using the Formula palette.

The *arguments* for a function are the details you provide to tell Excel what numbers to calculate with that function. They appear inside parentheses following the function's name, like this: =SUM(C1:C6). In this case, the range C1:C6 is the argument for the SUM function. Some functions require several arguments to function correctly, and it's difficult to remember the exact arguments and entry order needed. The Formula palette helps by providing boxes you can fill in for each argument.

Using the Formula Palette with the SUM Function

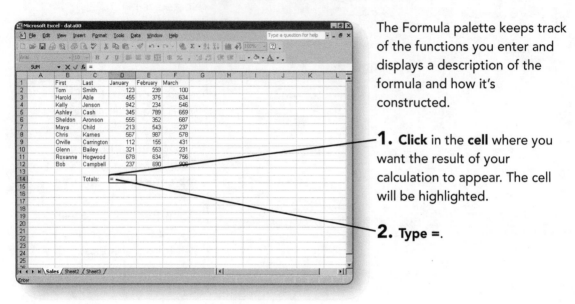

The Formula palette keeps track of the functions you enter and displays a description of the formula and how it's constructed.

1. Click in the **cell** where you want the result of your calculation to appear. The cell will be highlighted.

2. Type =.

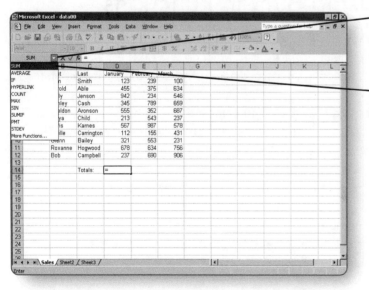

3. Click on the **down arrow** next to the Functions list. The list will drop down.

4. Click on **SUM**. The Formula palette will appear.

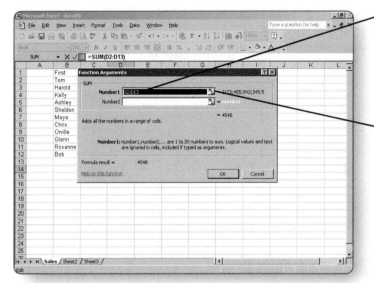

Notice that in the Number1 text box, Excel has tried to guess which numbers you're trying to add. If it is correct, you can skip steps 5 through 7.

5. Click on the **Collapse Dialog button** at the end of the Number1 text box to edit the formula. The Formula palette will shrink to allow you to see your worksheet and select the range of cells for the calculation.

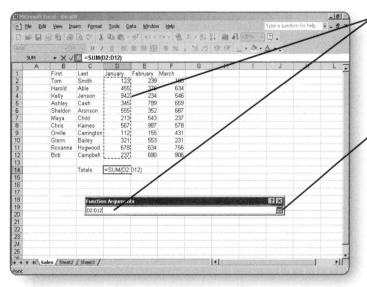

6. Select the **cells** to be included in your calculation. A marquee will highlight your selection, and a range will appear in the formula bar.

7. Click on the **Expand Dialog button**, or **press** the **Enter key**. The Formula palette will expand with your selection entered in the Number1 text box.

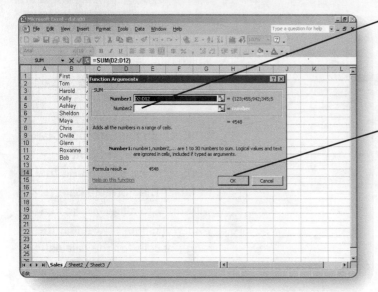

If you want to add another series of data or just another number to your calculation, click in the Number2 text box and repeat steps 5 through 7.

8. Click on **OK** if the calculation in the formula bar is correct. Your formula will be entered.

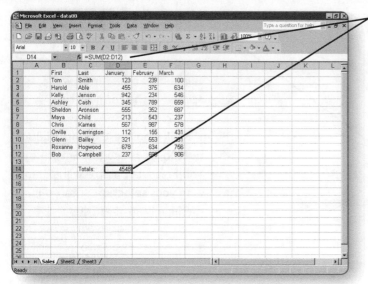

You can view the formula in the formula bar and the total of the calculation in the selected cell.

NOTE

You can copy the formula you just created to the other columns, and the copies will sum the numbers in their respective columns. See "Copying Formulas with Relative and Absolute References" later in this chapter.

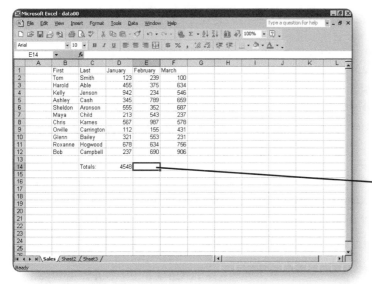

Using AutoSum

AutoSum is a shortcut method of summing a column or row of numbers. It is faster than the method you just learned, but it works only with the SUM function.

1. Click in the **cell** where you want a result. The cell will be highlighted.

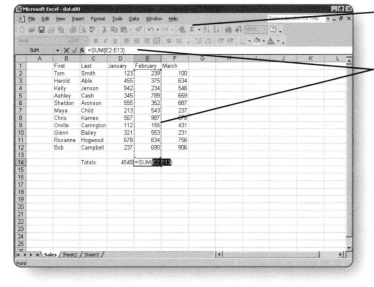

2. Click on the **AutoSum button**.

In the formula bar, Excel will suggest a range to be added. The suggested range of cells will appear with a marquee around it (a flashing dashed box).

3. Press the **Enter key** if the range Excel suggests is correct. The result of the AutoSum will be entered in the selected cell.

If the suggested range is not correct, use the mouse to select the range you want before pressing the Enter key.

Creating an IF Function

All functions work in basically the same way. You enter the equal sign, select the function, and then tell the function which data to use. The next example demonstrates using a logical function rather than a mathematical one. Logical functions use the =, >, <, >=, <=, and <> operators within a formula to test whether something is true or false.

If the function is true, one result is returned; if false, another is returned. In the following example, the formula returns "Yes" if the employee's quarterly total is more than 1200. It returns "No" if the amount is equal to or less than 1200.

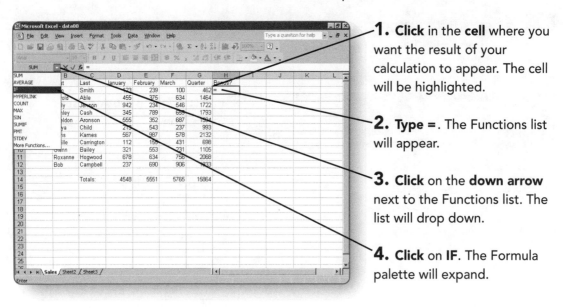

1. **Click** in the **cell** where you want the result of your calculation to appear. The cell will be highlighted.

2. **Type =**. The Functions list will appear.

3. **Click** on the **down arrow** next to the Functions list. The list will drop down.

4. **Click** on **IF**. The Formula palette will expand.

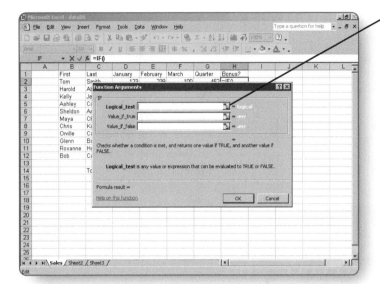

5. Click on the **Collapse Dialog button** at the end of the Logical test text box. The Formula palette will shrink.

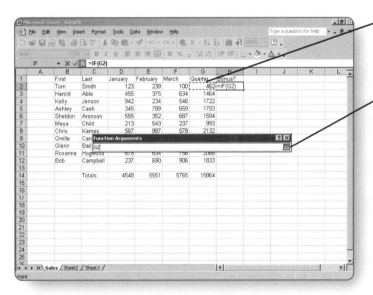

6. Select the **cell or cells** to evaluate. A flashing marquee will appear around the cell(s).

7. Click on the **Expand Dialog button** to expand the Formula palette. The selected range will be entered in the text box.

8. Type the **condition** in the Logical test text box. For example, to test whether the value is greater than 1200, type >1200.

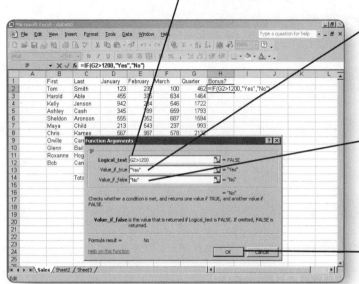

9. In the Value if true text box, **type** the **text** you want to appear if the condition is true. Include quotation marks around the text ("Yes").

10. In the Value if false text box, **type** the **text** you want returned if the condition is false. Include quotation marks around the text ("No").

11. Click on **OK**. The appropriate text will appear in the cell, and the formula you entered will appear in the formula bar.

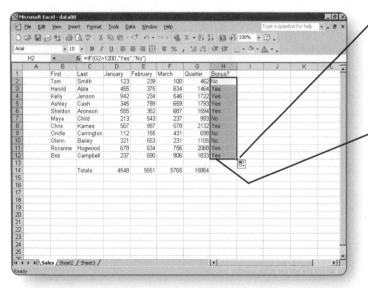

12. Drag the **Fill handle** across a row or column to copy the formula. Results of the same formula for each of the other rows will appear.

In rows where the value in column G is less than or equal to 1200, column H reports "No"; it shows "Yes" when the value is greater than 1200.

Copying Formulas with Relative and Absolute References

When you copy a formula, the copy changes depending on where you put it. It is therefore said to be *relative*. You saw this at work in the last two steps of the preceding procedure.

When you copied the formula from cell H2 into cells H3 through H12, the reference to cell G2 changed to refer to cells G3 through G12, respectively.

The formula in H2 refers to G2.

When that formula is copied to cell H10, it refers to cell G10.

Most of the time you will want Excel to copy formulas in this way. However, there may be times when you want an *absolute* cell reference, which does not change depending on location.

Suppose, for example, that you want to include a reference to a particular cell in multiple formulas. You could write a formula that marks that cell reference as an absolute value by placing dollar signs in front of the column letter and row number. The reference to that cell will then stay fixed (absolute) when you copy the formula elsewhere.

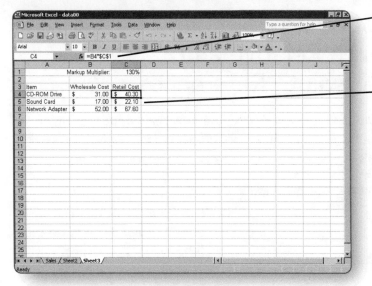

This cell's formula multiplies the number in B4 by the multiplier in C1.

This cell's formula takes the value in column C of its own row (C5) and multiplies it by C1. Because C1 appears as C1 in the formula, the reference does not change when the formula is copied to different locations.

To set up a formula like the one in the preceding example, use the following procedure.

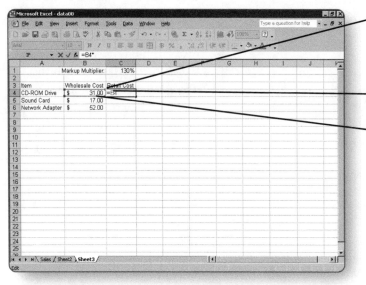

1. **Click** in the **cell** where you want the formula. The cell will be highlighted.

2. **Type =** .

3. **Click** on the **cell** that you want to use for the first part of the formula. This is the cell that will change when you copy the formula.

4. **Type** a **math operator symbol** to indicate the math operator you want.

5. **Type** $ (a dollar sign).

6. **Type** the **column letter** for the cell that should have an absolute reference.

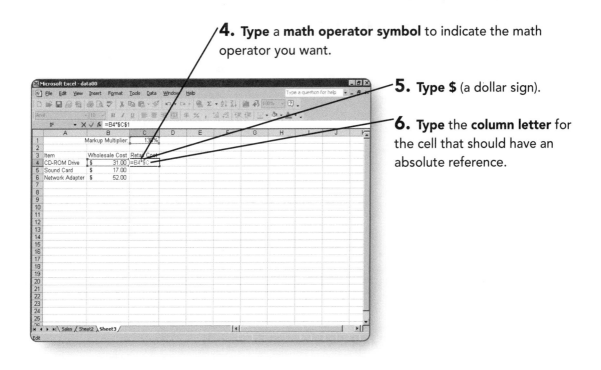

7. **Type another** $.

8. **Type** the **row number** for the cell that should have an absolute reference.

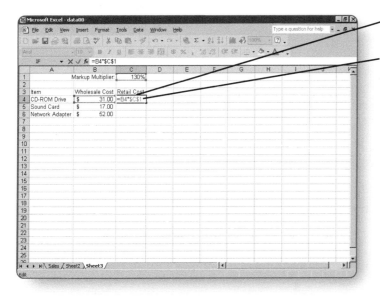

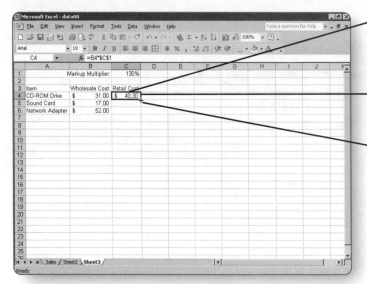

9. Press the **Enter key**. The formula result will appear in the cell.

10. Click on the **cell** containing the formula again to reselect it.

11. Point at the **Fill handle** in the lower-right corner of the selected cell. The mouse pointer will become a cross.

> ### NOTE
>
> When you are creating or editing a formula, position your insertion point within a cell reference and then press F4 to cycle through the available combinations of relative and absolute references. For example, if the reference is to cell C1, pressing the F4 key produces C1, C$1, and $C1, sequentially. Stop pressing F4 when the value you want appears.

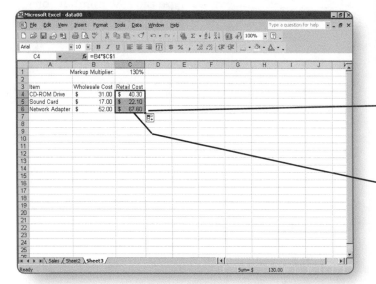

12. Drag the **Fill handle** to highlight the cells where you want to copy the formula.

The copied formulas have different values for the first cell reference, but they all have C1 as the second cell reference.

Using AutoCalculate

You might find that occasionally you want to know the sum or average of a group of numbers but don't really need to record the information in a worksheet. By default, the sum of a group of selected cells appears automatically in the status bar, but you can change that to Average, Count, or one of several other common calculations.

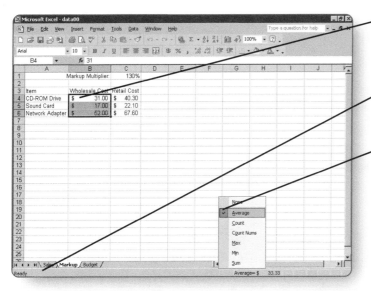

1. Select the **cells** containing the values you want to calculate. The cells will be highlighted.

2. Right-click on the **status bar**. A pop-up menu will appear.

3. Click on a **function** to put a check mark by it. The result of the calculation will appear in the status bar.

Inserting Today's Date

In Excel, dates are stored numerically so that you can perform calculations on them. For example, you might subtract today's date from January 1, 2001 to calculate how many days have elapsed since then. Since raw numbers are difficult to read as dates, Excel provides a Date format for numbers that displays the date equivalent to the number in a cell.

Excel has a special function for inserting today's date. It pulls the date from your computer's built-in clock/calendar and inserts it in the active cell.

1. **Click** on the **cell** in which you want to insert the date. The cell will be highlighted.

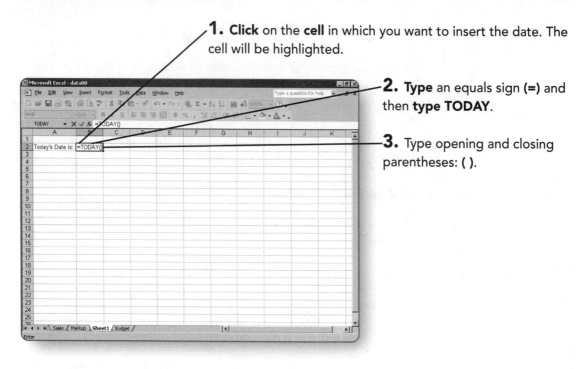

2. **Type** an equals sign **(=)** and then **type TODAY**.

3. Type opening and closing parentheses: **( )**.

4. **Press Enter**. Today's date will appear in the cell.

5. **Click** on **Format**. The Format menu will open.

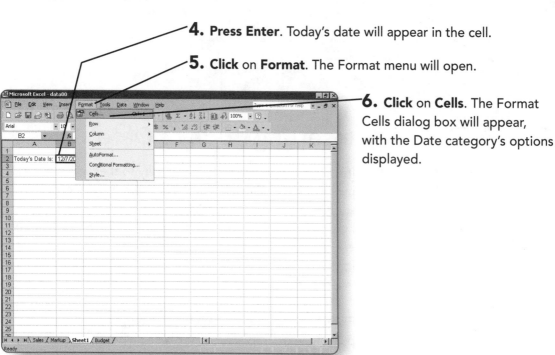

6. **Click** on **Cells**. The Format Cells dialog box will appear, with the Date category's options displayed.

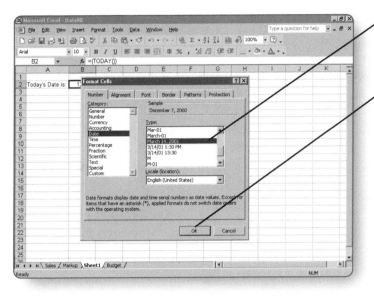

7. Click on the **date format** you want on the Type list. The format will be highlighted.

8. Click on **OK**. The chosen format will be applied to the date.

Some Common Mistakes to Avoid

The Formula palette helps beginners avoid mistakes, but you'll probably still make a few. When you make a mistake, a number of error messages might appear. The following are the most common:

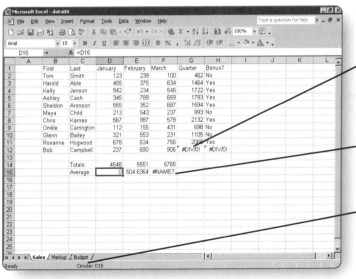

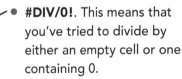

- **#DIV/0!**. This means that you've tried to divide by either an empty cell or one containing 0.

- **#NAME?**. This may mean that you deleted information referred to in your formula.

- **Circular**. This means that a formula in a cell refers to the same cell. You may see a blue dot in a cell containing a circular reference.

When you check your formulas, some things to watch for are that:

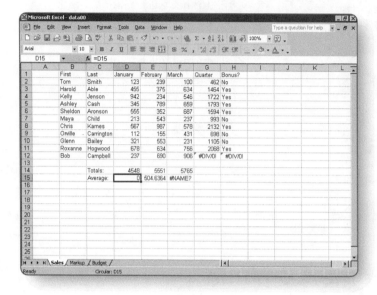

- Formulas start with an equals sign.

- All the necessary parentheses are included.

- You referred to the correct cells.

- You've included all the arguments for a function and no extra arguments.

NOTE

You may find the Auditing toolbar handy in resolving worksheet errors. To display it, open the Tools menu, point to Auditing, and click on Show Auditing Toolbar. For more information about the tools on this toolbar, press Shift+F1 and then click on the tool for a more detailed explanation of it.

7

Navigating Your Worksheets

As you create larger worksheets, it's possible to get lost in the flood of data and not know exactly where you are. Fortunately, Excel has features to help you work with larger worksheets. In this chapter, you'll learn how to:

- Name a range
- Move directly to a specific cell or range
- Find and replace entries in your worksheet
- Hide and display rows and columns
- Split your Excel window and freeze parts of a worksheet

Naming a Range

Naming a range is useful because names are easier to read and remember than cell addresses. Named ranges can be used to quickly select text and move around a worksheet in combination with the Go To command. They can also be used in formulas.

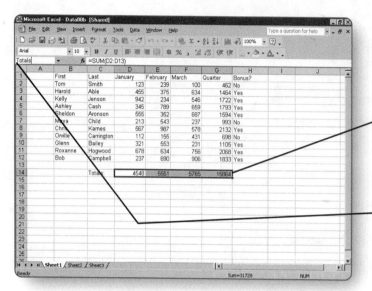

1. **Click** in a **cell** or **drag** the **mouse pointer** across a range of cells. The cell(s) will be highlighted.

2. **Click** in the **Name text box** to the left of the formula bar. The text box will be highlighted.

3. **Type** a **name** for the highlighted cells.

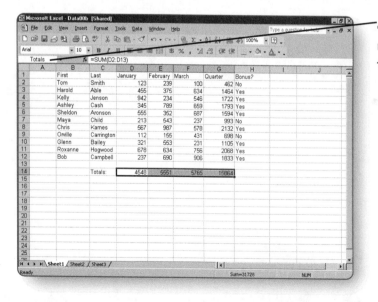

4. **Press** the **Enter key**. The name will appear in the Name text box.

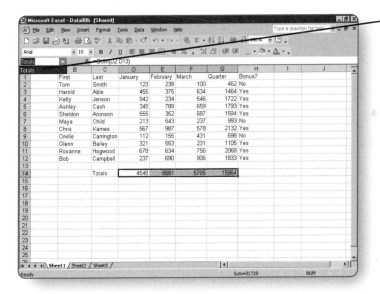

To quickly select a named cell or range, click on the down arrow at the end of the Name text box and select from the drop-down list.

You can also name entire rows and columns, and then use those names to find the value contained in the cell at their intersection. For example, suppose that you named column D "January" and row 2 "Smith."

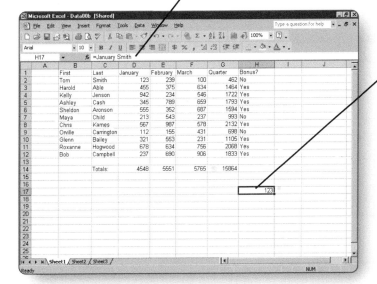

You could then enter the formula **=January Smith** anywhere in the worksheet and it would pull the value from cell D2. (The space between January and Smith is called the intersection operator.) Such formulas are absolute and do not change when you move or copy them.

Moving Directly to a Cell or Range

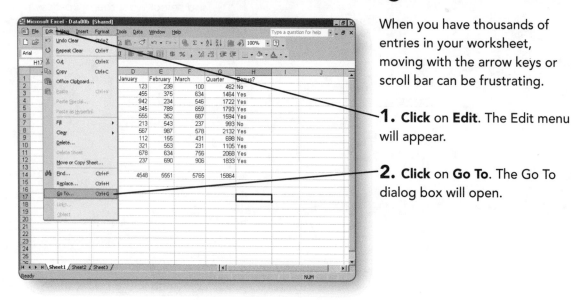

When you have thousands of entries in your worksheet, moving with the arrow keys or scroll bar can be frustrating.

1. Click on **Edit**. The Edit menu will appear.

2. Click on **Go To**. The Go To dialog box will open.

3a. Type a **cell address** or **range name** in the Reference text box.

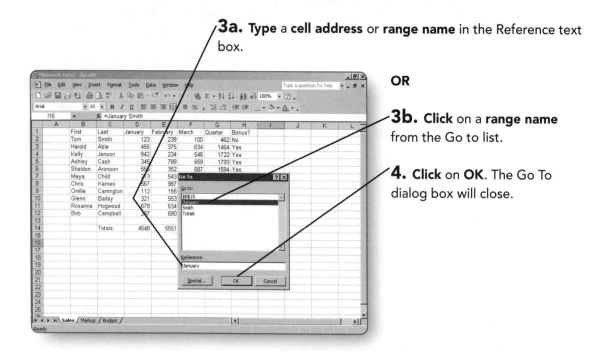

OR

3b. Click on a **range name** from the Go to list.

4. Click on **OK**. The Go To dialog box will close.

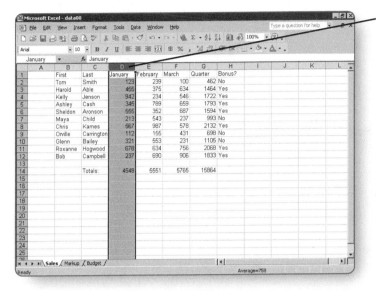

The cell or range you specified will become the active cell or selected range.

TIP

To move to the last cell that contains data in a worksheet, press the Ctrl and End keys at the same time. To move back to the first cell (A1), press the Ctrl and Home keys at the same time.

Finding and Replacing Cell Entries

If you need to update your worksheet (maybe interest rates have increased), you can use the Find or Replace commands to help you.

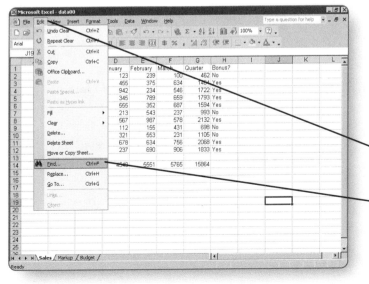

Finding Cell Entries

To modify data in your worksheet, you must first find the cell (or cells) that contains the data you want to change.

1. Click on **Edit**. The Edit menu will appear.

2. Click on **Find**. The Find dialog box will open.

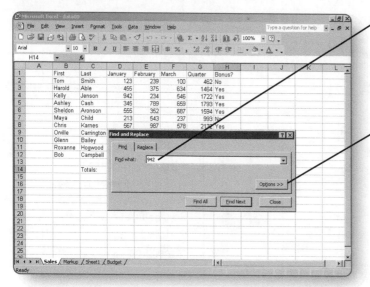

3. **Type** the **word** or **number** you want to find in the Find what text box. Be sure to enter it exactly as it was originally entered into the worksheet.

4. **Click** on the **Options button**. Extra Find controls will appear in the dialog box.

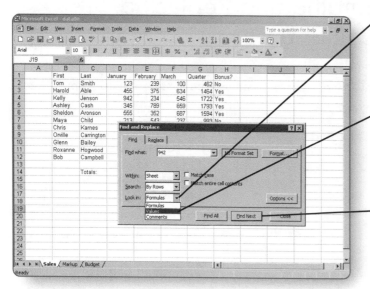

5. **Click** on the **down arrow** next to the Look in text box. The Look in drop-down list will appear.

6. **Click** on **Formulas**, **Values**, or **Comments**, depending on what kind of data you want Find to search.

7. **Click** on **Find Next**.

Excel will find the first occurrence of the word or number. You can continue to click on Find Next until all occurrences have been identified.

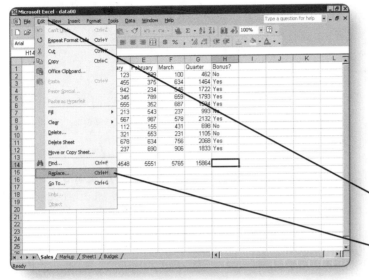

Replacing Cell Entries

When a cell that needs to be modified is found, you can use Excel to automatically replace the data for you without your having to manually enter the changes.

1. Click on **Edit**. The Edit menu will appear.

2. Click on **Replace**. The Replace dialog box will open.

3. Type the **word** or **number** you want to replace in the Find what text box.

4. Type the **revised entry** in the Replace with text box.

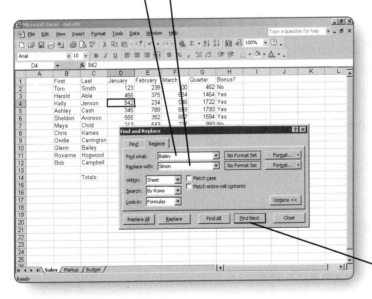

NOTE

At this point, you can click on Replace All and immediately replace all occurrences of the original entry with the new one. However, it's not a good idea to do this if you're not an experienced user. You may replace something you didn't intend to replace.

5. Click on **Find Next**. Excel will find the first occurrence of the word or number.

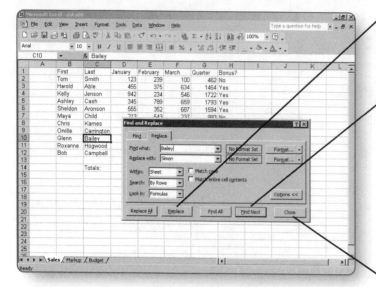

6a. **Click** on **Replace**. The item will be replaced.

OR

6b. **Click** on **Find Next**. Excel will find the next occurrence of the word or number.

7. **Repeat steps 5 and 6** until you've checked all occurrences of the word or number in the worksheet.

8. **Click** on **Close**. The dialog box will close.

Viewing Different Parts of Your Worksheet at the Same Time

When your worksheet is bigger than the area you can see on your screen at one time, it becomes difficult to remember where exactly you are as you move down or across a worksheet and can no longer see the row and column labels you entered. Are you in the January or February column, or the cash or sales row? You can manipulate a worksheet in several ways to overcome this problem.

Hiding Rows and Columns

If your worksheet has columns or rows that you really don't need to work in anymore, or that you don't want to print, you can hide them.

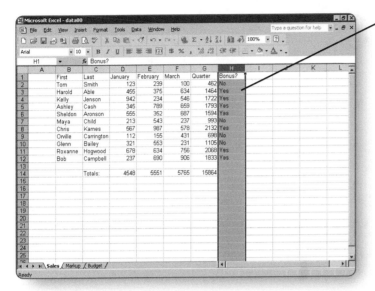

1. Select the **column** or **row** to hide. The column or row will be highlighted.

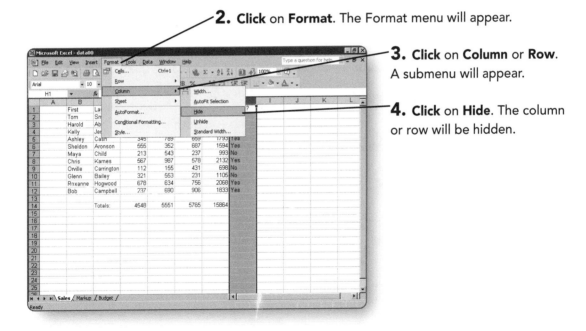

2. Click on **Format**. The Format menu will appear.

3. Click on **Column** or **Row**. A submenu will appear.

4. Click on **Hide**. The column or row will be hidden.

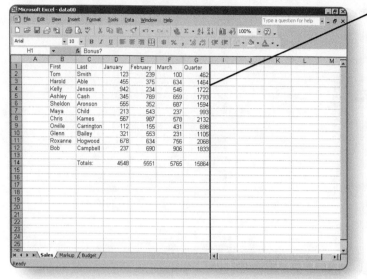

Initially, a dark vertical or horizontal line will appear where the columns or rows you have hidden were. This is the hidden column or row, still selected.

However, once you move in the worksheet, the dark line disappears and the only way to tell that rows or columns have been hidden is by the missing letters or numbers in the row or column headers.

Displaying Hidden Rows or Columns

If you decide you do need to see those hidden rows or columns, you can make them reappear in the worksheet.

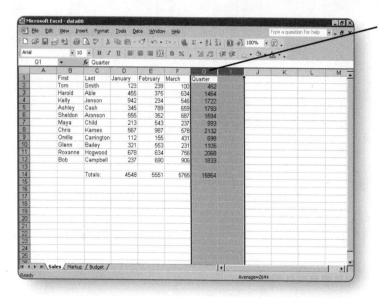

1. Select the **rows** or **columns** on both sides of the missing rows or columns. The cells will be highlighted.

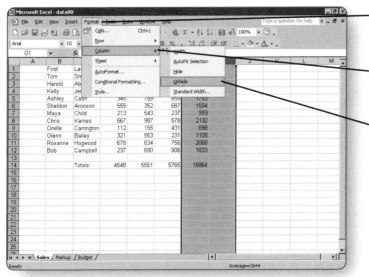

2. Click on **Format**. The Format menu will appear.

3. Click on **Column** or **Row**. A submenu will appear.

4. Click on **Unhide**.

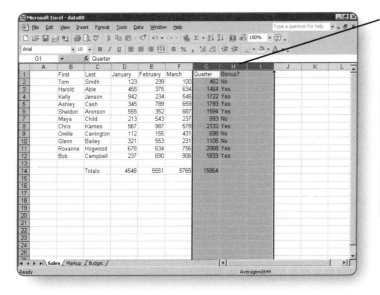

The missing columns or rows will reappear.

TIP

You can also hide a column or row by selecting it and then right-clicking on it. Choose Hide from the shortcut menu that will appear.

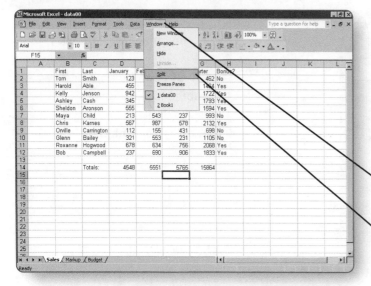

Splitting a Window

If you want to see particular sections of the same worksheet, but the worksheet is so big that you can't view both sections on-screen at the same time, you can split a window.

1. Click on **Window**. The Window menu will appear.

2. Click on **Split**. The spreadsheet will be divided into four panes.

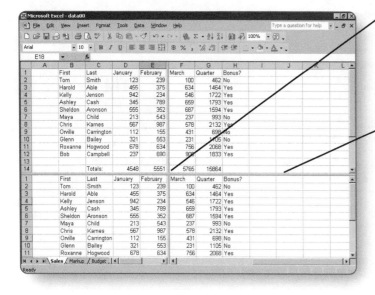

When you split the window, each pane has its own scroll bars. You can scroll each pane and/or drag the split bars to reposition them on the screen.

3. Adjust the **view** of your worksheet in each pane with the four scroll bars until you can see what you want to compare.

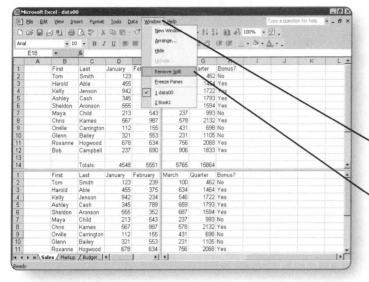

Removing a Split

If you no longer need the split view, you can remove the split so that your screen shows only one section of the worksheet.

1. Click on **Window**. The Window menu will appear.

2. Click on **Remove Split**. The split will be removed.

Keeping Row or Column Labels Visible

When you're entering data, you need to know which row and column you're on. The letters and numbers Excel provides are not very informative. You need to be able to see the labels you set up for certain columns and rows, such as months of the year or employee names. You can do this by freezing columns and rows that contain labels you need to see all the time.

1. Click in the **cell** below the column labels and to the right of the row labels. The cell will be highlighted.

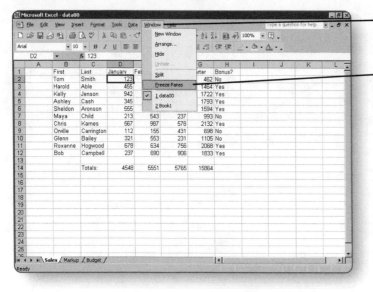

2. Click on **Window**. The Window menu will appear.

3. Click on **Freeze Panes**. The column and row labels will stay on-screen while you work with the spreadsheet.

Removing the Freeze

If you do not need to see column and row labels all the time, you can remove the freeze so that the column and row labels scroll as usual.

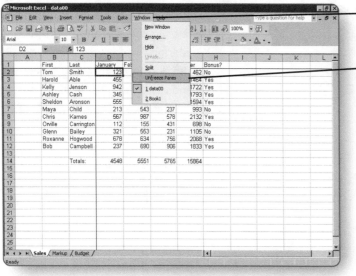

1. Click on **Window**. The Window menu will appear.

2. Click on **Unfreeze Panes**. The column and row labels will now move as you work with the spreadsheet.

8

Working with Data

Excel can be used not only to perform calculations but also to store data that you can then sort and filter to find information and make decisions. In this chapter, you'll learn how to:

- Sort data by rows and columns
- Filter for information that meets specific criteria

Sorting Data

If you enter a large amount of data into a worksheet, it may be easier to find information you need by sorting your data. You can easily sort data in Excel either alphabetically or numerically, in ascending or descending order.

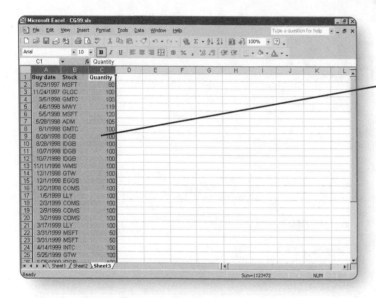

Sorting the Order of Rows in a Range

1a. Click and **drag** the **mouse pointer** to highlight the cells of the range you want to sort. Any cells outside the selected range will not be included in the sort.

OR

1b. Move the insertion point into any cell in the range to be sorted. The entire range adjacent to the active cell will be used for the sort.

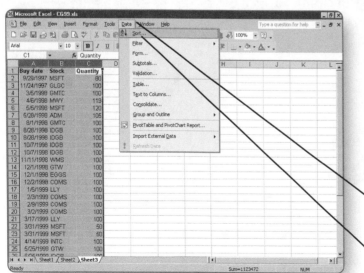

NOTE

If you select only a single column in step 1a, a confirmation box appears asking whether you really intend to sort only that column.

2. Click on **Data**. The Data menu will appear.

3. Click on **Sort**. The Sort dialog box will open.

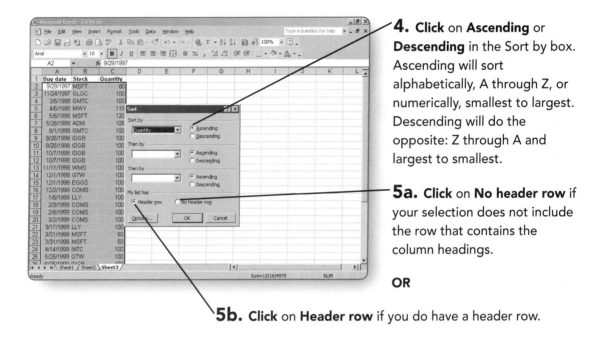

4. **Click** on **Ascending** or **Descending** in the Sort by box. Ascending will sort alphabetically, A through Z, or numerically, smallest to largest. Descending will do the opposite: Z through A and largest to smallest.

5a. **Click** on **No header row** if your selection does not include the row that contains the column headings.

OR

5b. **Click** on **Header row** if you do have a header row.

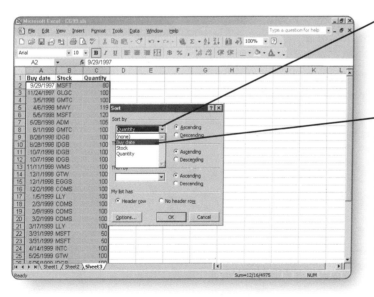

6. **Click** on the **down arrow** next to the Sort by drop-down list. The list of options to sort by will appear.

7. **Click** on the **name of the column** by which you want to sort. If you chose Header row in step 5, the names of the headers will appear on this drop-down list; if you chose No header row, the column letters will appear.

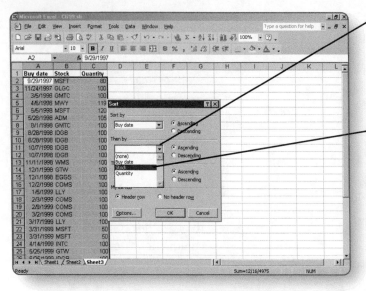

8. Click on the **down arrow** next to the Then by list if you want to sort by another column in the event of a duplicate value in the primary sort column.

9. Click on the **name of the column** to use for the secondary sort.

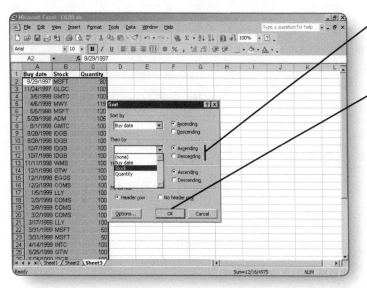

10. Click on **Ascending** or **Descending** for the secondary sort.

11. Click on **OK**. The dialog box will close.

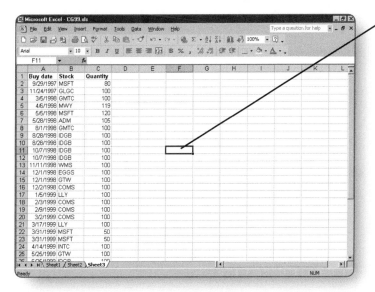

12. **Click** on a **spot** away from the selection area to deselect the cells. The data will be sorted according to the criteria you specified.

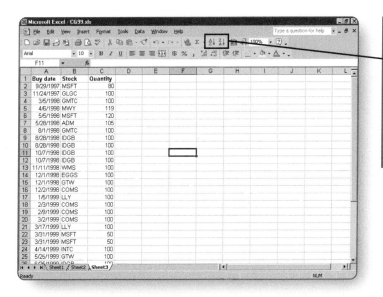

TIP

You can also sort using the Sort Ascending and Sort Descending toolbar buttons to sort by the column that contains the cell cursor.

Sorting the Order of Columns in a Range

The following steps change the order of the columns from left to right, without affecting the order in which the records (the rows) appear.

1. Click and **drag** the **mouse pointer** to highlight the cells of the range you want to sort.

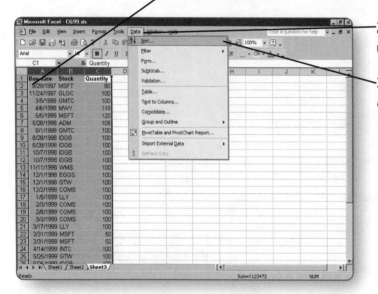

2. Click on **Data**. The Data menu will appear.

3. Click on **Sort**. The Sort dialog box will open.

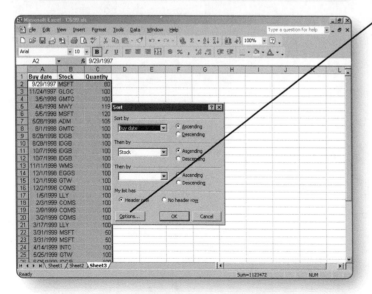

4. Click on **Options**. The Sort Options dialog box will open.

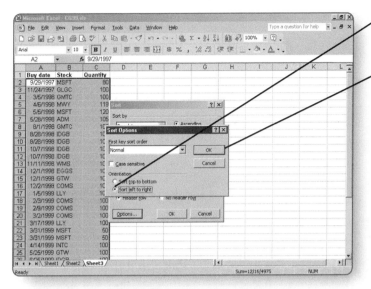

5. Click on **Sort left to right** in the Orientation section.

6. Click on **OK**. The Sort Options dialog box will close, and you will be returned to the Sort dialog box.

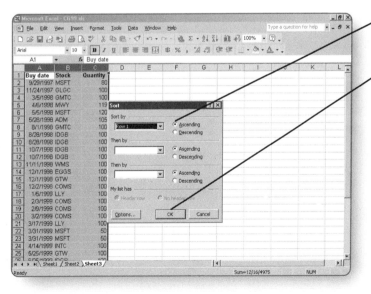

7. Click on **Ascending** in the Sort by box.

8. Click on **OK**. The Sort dialog box will close.

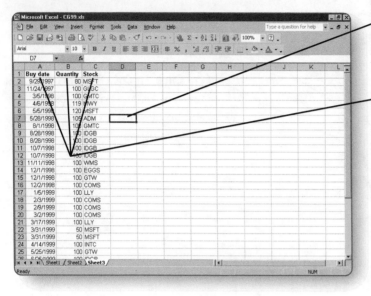

9. **Click anywhere** away from the selected range. The cells will be deselected.

The data will appear sorted alphabetically by column head, left to right.

Filtering Data

You can search for data using the Filter command to select information that meets criteria of your choosing. For example, you can set up a filter that will find dates that come after 01/01/99.

1. **Click** on the **column head** that you want to use in your search. The cell will be highlighted.

2. **Click** on **Data**. The Data menu will appear.

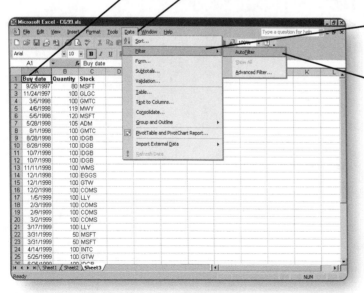

3. **Click** on **Filter**. A submenu will appear.

4. **Click** on **AutoFilter**. AutoFilter arrows will appear next to the column heads.

You can filter by any field, but for this example, the criterion you will set is Buy date is greater than 01/01/99.

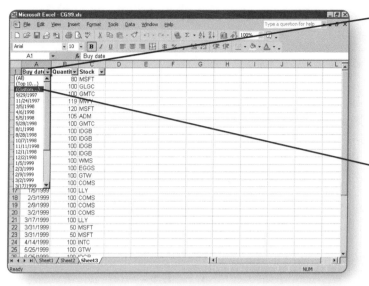

5. **Click** on the **down arrow** in the column for Buy date. All the entries in the Buy date column will appear in the drop-down list. You can select any of the options in the list to see only those rows in the worksheet.

6. **Click** on **Custom**. A criterion for selecting rows in the worksheet will be set up. The Custom AutoFilter dialog box will open.

7. **Click** on the **down arrow** next to the left field. A drop-down list will appear.

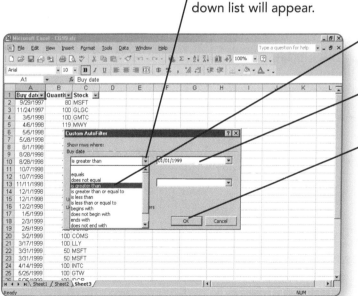

8. **Click** on **is greater than**. Your selection will be highlighted.

9. **Tab** to the **next text box** to the right and **type 01/01/1999**.

10. **Click** on **OK**.

TIP

You can continue to refine your requirements in the Custom AutoFilter dialog box. For example, you could search for greater than 01/01/99 and less than 12/01/99 using "And" with the additional text boxes.

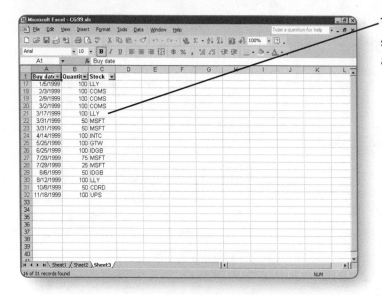

The worksheet will now only show transactions that occurred after 01/01/99.

Turning Off AutoFilter

When you are finished using AutoFilter, it's easy to turn it off.

1. Click on **Data**. The Data menu will appear.

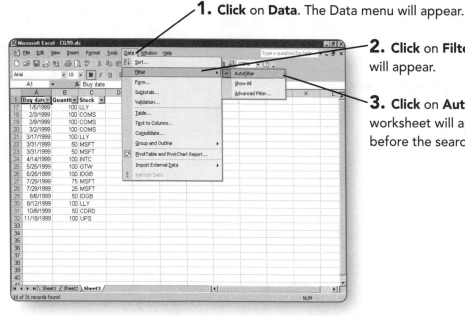

2. Click on **Filter**. A submenu will appear.

3. Click on **AutoFilter**. The worksheet will appear as it was before the search.

9

Working with Templates

Templates are built-in forms that enable you to produce professional-looking documents such as invoices with just a few keystrokes. In this chapter, you'll learn how to:

- Create a new workbook with a template
- Edit a template
- Change the settings for new blank workbooks

Creating a New Workbook with a Template

Excel comes with several templates, such as Balance Sheet, Expense Statement, and Timecard. Each template provides formatting and sample text and formulas for a particular task. Microsoft collectively calls the Excel templates *Spreadsheet Solutions*.

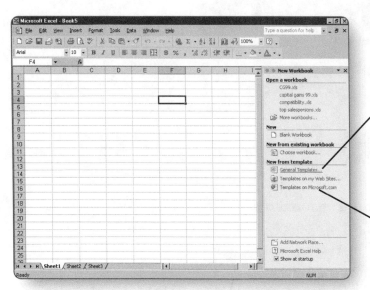

1. Click on **General Templates** in the task pane. The Templates dialog box will open.

NOTE

You can also download other templates from Microsoft's Web site. To do so, click the Templates on Microsoft.com hyperlink in the task pane.

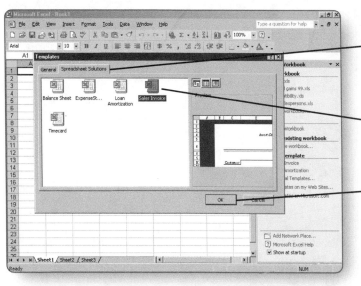

2. Click on **Spreadsheet Solutions**. That tab's content will appear.

3. Click on the **template** you want to use. The template's icon will be highlighted.

4. Click on **OK**. Excel will open a new workbook based on that template.

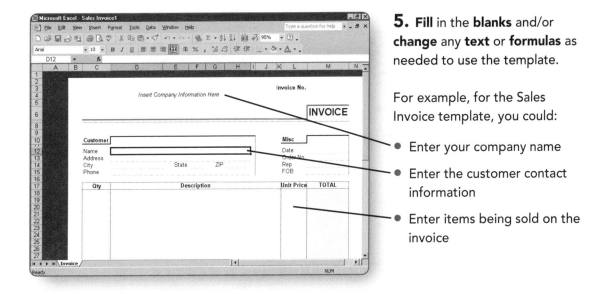

5. Fill in the **blanks** and/or **change** any **text** or **formulas** as needed to use the template.

For example, for the Sales Invoice template, you could:

- Enter your company name
- Enter the customer contact information
- Enter items being sold on the invoice

Modifying a Template

Sometimes you might need to modify the template itself. For example, you might want to modify the Sales Invoice template so that your company's name appears on it each time without your having to retype it.

TIP

Instead of modifying the original templates that come with Excel, it's better to save the changes under a different name. That way you can go back to the unaltered version of the original if needed, while still enjoying your customized version.

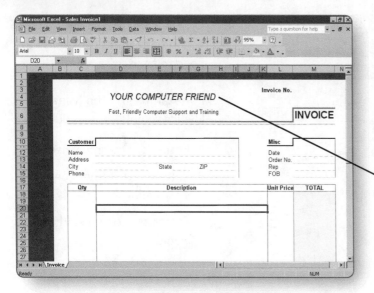

1. Create a **new workbook** using a template, as in the preceding section.

2. Make any **changes** that you want to appear on the modified template.

For example, you might enter your company name and motto and apply formatting to the text.

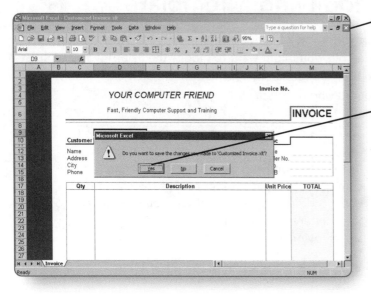

3. Click the **Close (X) button** for the workbook. A dialog box will open asking whether you want to save your changes.

4. Click on **Yes**.

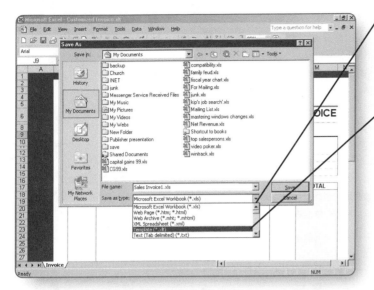

5. Click on the **down-pointing arrow** next to the Save as type box. A list of file types will appear.

6. Click on **Template (*.xlt).** Template will appear in the Save as type box, and the Save in location will change to the default storage location for user-created templates.

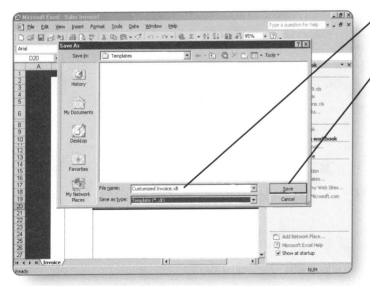

7. Type a **name** for the new template in the File name box.

8. Click on **Save.** The workbook will close and your changes will be saved to a new template.

TIP

The default storage location for user-created templates is C:\Windows\Application Data\Microsoft\Templates if you are using Windows 95/98/Me, or C:\Documents and Settings*user_name*\Application Data\Microsoft\Templates if you are using Windows 2000. The default storage location for the templates that actually come with Excel 10 is C:\Program Files\Microsoft Office\Templates\1033. If you store a template in either of these locations, it will appear in the Templates dialog box when you start a new workbook based on a template.

TIP

You can turn any workbook into a template simply by saving it as a template, just as you did with the workbook in the preceding section that was based on one of Excel's own Spreadsheet Solutions template. A template need not be limited to boilerplate text; you might set up a workbook with certain default fonts, certain page header and footer information, an alternate print layout, or other specifications.

Modifying the Default Workbook Settings

When you create a new, blank workbook using the New button on the toolbar, or using the Blank Workbook hyperlink in the task pane, the new workbook is based on internal settings in Excel. You can override these settings, however, by creating a template called *Book* and placing it in the C:\Program Files\Microsoft Office\Office\XLStart folder. From then on, all new workbooks will use the settings contained in Book.xlt instead of the internal settings.

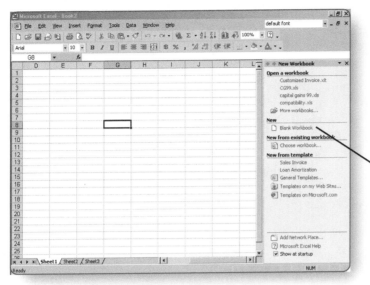

For example, the following steps show how to create a Book.xlt file that specifies a different default column width. You can substitute any other formatting you would like for steps 2 through 5.

1. Click on the **Blank Workbook hyperlink** on the task pane, starting a new workbook.

2. Click on **Format**. The Format menu will appear.

3. Point to **Column**. The Column submenu will appear.

4. Click on **Standard Width**. The Standard Width dialog box will open.

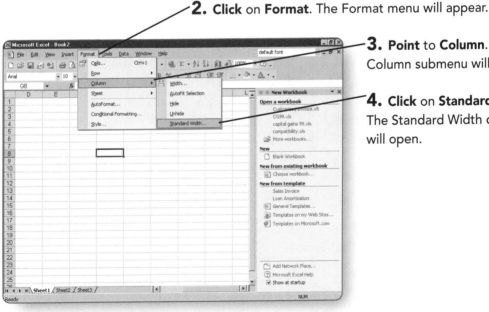

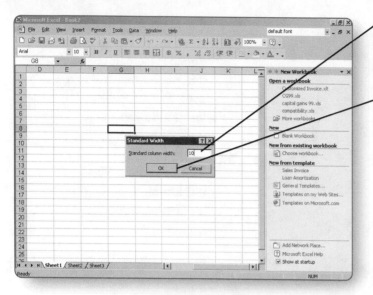

5. **Type** a **new column width**, such as 10, in the Standard column width text box.

6. **Click** on **OK**. All the columns in the workbook will change to the new standard width.

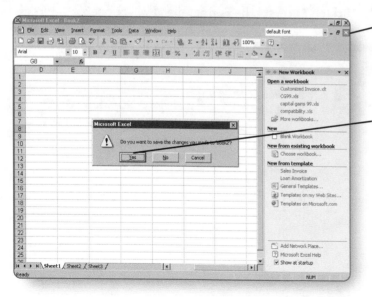

7. **Click** on the **Close (X) button** for the workbook. A dialog box will ask whether you want to save your changes.

8. **Click** on **Yes**. The Save As dialog box will open.

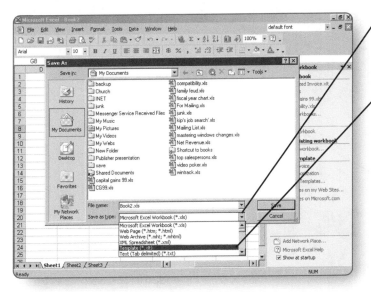

9. Click on the **down arrow** next to Save as type. A list of file types will appear.

10. Click on **Template (*.xlt)**. Template will appear as the file type.

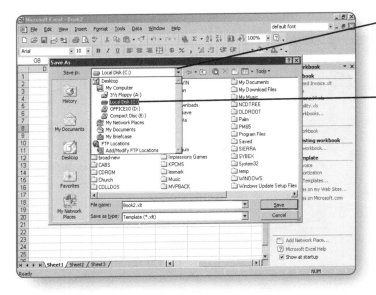

11. Click on the **down arrow** next to the Save in box. A list of locations will appear.

12. Click on the **C drive**. A list of folders on the C drive will appear.

13. Double-click the **following folders**, in turn:

- Program Files
- Microsoft Office
- Office
- XLStart

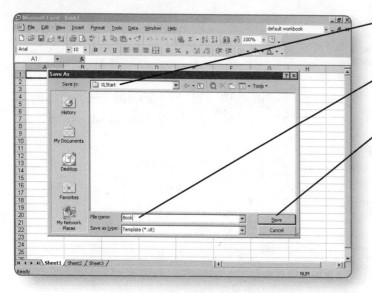

When you finish, XLStart will appear in the Save in box.

14. **Type Book** in the File name box.

15. **Click** on **Save**. The template will be saved.

16. **Click** on the **New button** on the toolbar to start a new, blank workbook.

Notice that the default column width for the new workbook is the amount you specified in Book.xlt.

10

Exploring Print Options

Although you can send your worksheets directly to paper by clicking on File, and then Print, as described in Chapter 3, "Saving, Printing, and Exiting Excel," other options are available. These options not only make your documents look more professional but also save you time and money by letting you see exactly what you're going to print before you use any paper. In this chapter, you'll learn how to:

- Set paper size, paper orientation, and margins
- Add headers and footers
- Select rows and columns to print on every page
- Select the print area
- Preview your document
- Set page breaks

Setting Paper Size and Orientation

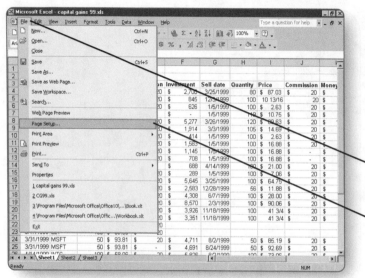

Unlike letters, which are always printed using Portrait orientation, some worksheets may look better printed using Landscape orientation. You'll need to make decisions about how your printouts will look.

1. Click on **File**. The File menu will appear.

2. Click on **Page Setup**. The Page Setup dialog box will open.

3. Click on the **Page tab**. In this tab, you can:

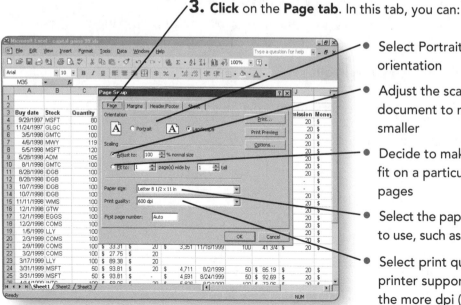

- Select Portrait or Landscape orientation

- Adjust the scaling of your document to make it larger or smaller

- Decide to make a worksheet fit on a particular number of pages

- Select the paper size you want to use, such as Letter or Legal

- Select print quality, if your printer supports this option; the more dpi (dots per inch), the better the quality

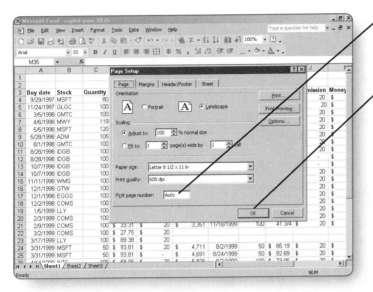

● Select the first page number to print, if you don't want to start at 1

4a. **Click** on **OK**. Your selections will be saved, and the Page Setup dialog box will close.

OR

4b. **Click** on **another tab** to get more options.

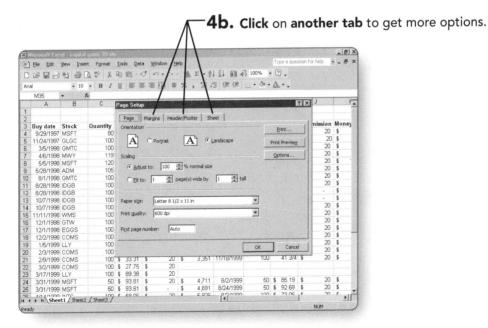

Setting Margins

To adjust your margins, click on File, and then Page Setup to open the Page Setup dialog box, if it's not already open.

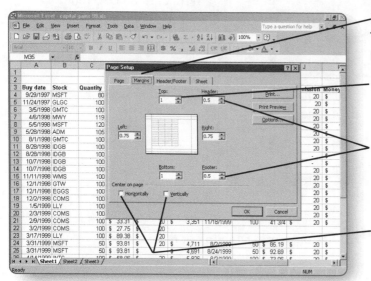

1. Click on the **Margins tab**. The tab will come to the front. In this tab, you can:

- Adjust the top, bottom, left, and right margins using the up and down arrows

- Adjust where the header and footer appear on a page by clicking on the up and down arrows

- Select to center a document either horizontally, vertically, or both

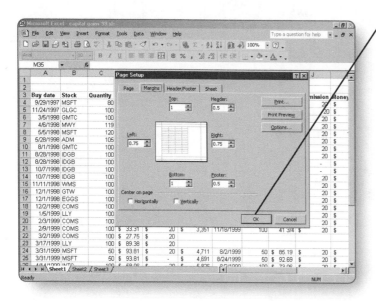

2a. Click on **OK**. Your selections will be saved, and the Page Setup dialog box will close.

OR

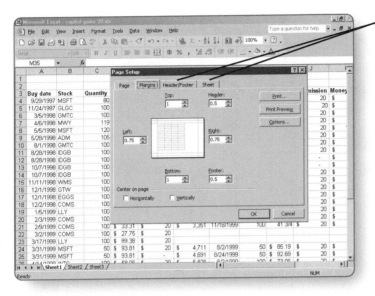

2b. **Click** on **another tab** to get more options.

Adding Headers and Footers

Headers and *footers* are simply text that appears either at the top (header) or bottom (footer) of every page. The types of information typically included in headers and footers are report titles, dates, page numbers, or file names.

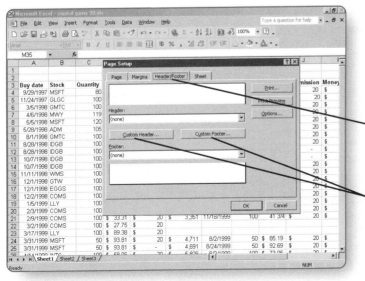

To add headers and footers, click on File, and then Page Setup to open the Page Setup dialog box, if it's not already open.

1. **Click** on the **Header/Footer tab**. The tab will come to the front.

2. **Click** on **Custom Header** or **Custom Footer**. The Header or Footer dialog box will open.

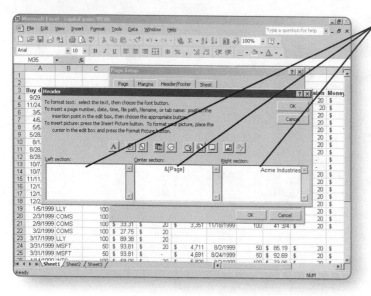

3. Click in the **Left**, **Center**, or **Right section text box**. This will determine where the text you insert will appear: left, right, or centered on the printed page.

If desired, click on the A button to open a Font dialog box, where you can change the font for the header or footer. Then click OK to return here.

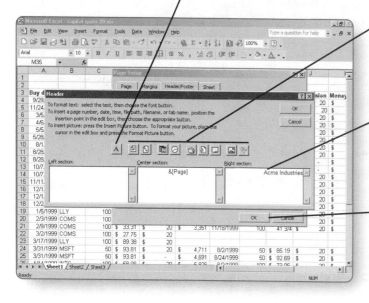

4. Insert a **page number**, **date**, **time**, **file name**, or **tab name** in a text box by clicking on the appropriate button.

5. Type any text that you want to appear in the header or footer in the appropriate text box.

6. Click on **OK**. The Header/Footer tab will reappear.

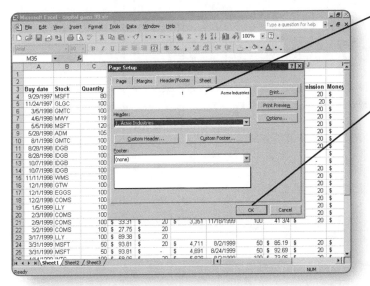

Notice that you will see a preview of how the header or footer will appear in the Header/Footer tab.

7a. Click on **OK**. Your selections will be saved, and the Page Setup dialog box will close.

OR

7b. Click on **another tab** to get more options.

Selecting Rows and Columns to Appear on Every Page

The final tab in the Page Setup dialog box is the Sheet tab. From here, you can make a number of choices including selecting rows or columns, which contain headings or labels, to repeat on every page.

First, click on File, and then Page Setup to open the Page Setup dialog box, if it's not already open.

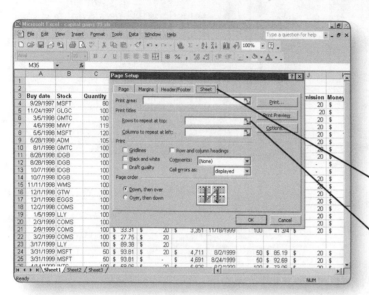

1. Click on the **Sheet tab**. The tab will come to the front.

2. Click on the **Collapse Dialog button** at the end of either the Rows to repeat at top or Columns to repeat at left text box. The Page Setup dialog box will shrink to reveal the worksheet.

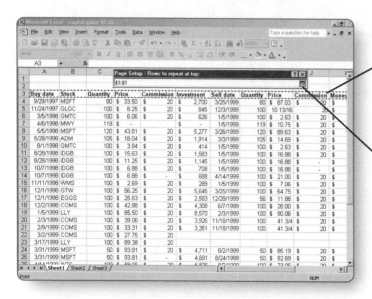

3. Select the **cells** you want to appear on each page. A marquee will appear around the highlighted cells.

4. Click on the **Expand Dialog button**. The Page Setup dialog box will reopen. The range will be automatically entered in the correct Print titles text box.

Other options in the Sheet tab you can select are:

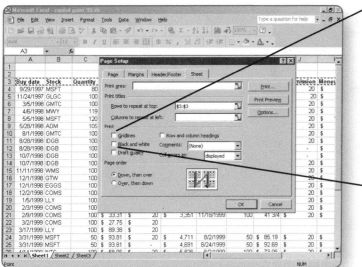

- **Gridlines**. Your printout will have the same grid as your worksheet does on the screen. If you don't select this option, there are no lines separating the rows and columns on the printout, even though you see them on the screen.

- **Black and white**. This will save the ink in your color printing cartridge, if you have one. Color cartridges are usually more expensive than black and white.

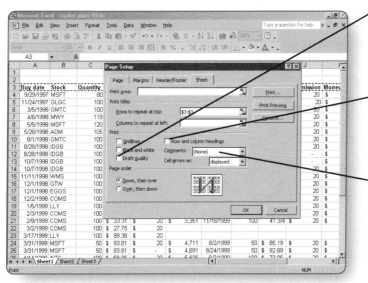

- **Draft quality**. Printing in draft quality is quicker, although the printout will not be quite as sharp.

- **Row and column headings**. Select row and column headings to print column letters and row numbers.

- **Comments**. You can choose to not print your comments by clicking on (None) from the drop-down list. You can also select to either print your comments at the end of the worksheet or as displayed on the sheet.

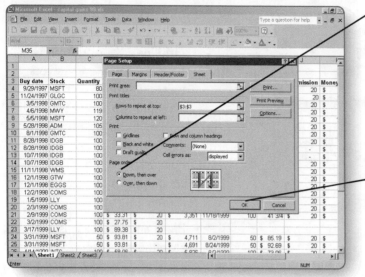

● **Page order.** If your work-sheet is both wider and longer than a single page, you can also choose whether to print pages down the worksheet before going across, or whether to go across first and then down.

5a. **Click** on **OK**. Your selections will be saved, and the Page Setup dialog box will close.

OR

5b. **Click** on **another tab** to get more options.

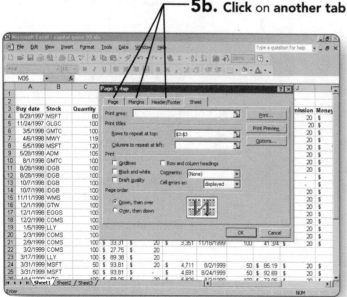

Setting the Print Area

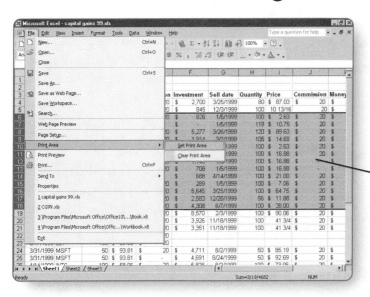

You may not want to print your entire worksheet. For example, you may have several years of data in the worksheet and you only want to print the information for one particular year.

1. **Click** and **drag** the **mouse pointer** over the area in the worksheet you want to print. The cells will be highlighted.

2. **Click** on **File**. The File menu will appear.

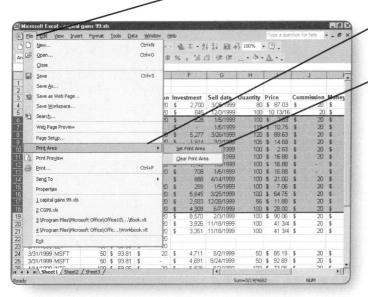

3. **Click** on **Print Area**. A submenu will appear.

4. **Click** on **Set Print Area**. The menu will disappear, and you will see a dotted line around the area you've selected. When you print now, only the print area will be printed.

Clearing the Print Area

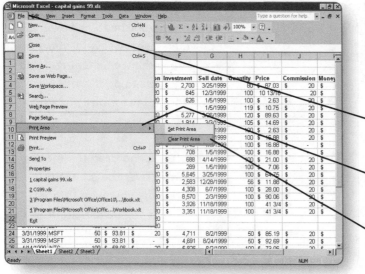

When you clear the print area, the whole sheet becomes reselected as the print area, so that when you print, the entire sheet prints.

1. Click on **File**. The File menu will appear.

2. Click on **Print Area**. A submenu will appear.

3. Click on **Clear Print Area**. The area will be cleared.

Previewing Your Worksheet

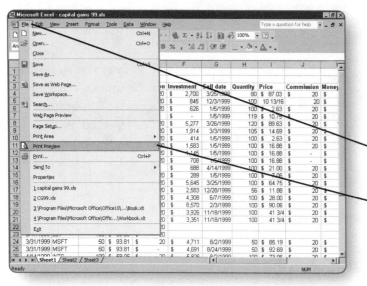

You'll probably save yourself a lot of paper if you always preview your worksheet to see what it looks like and check the margins before sending it to the printer.

1. Click on **File**. The File menu will appear.

2. Click on **Print Preview**. The Print Preview window will open.

Zooming

Depending on what you are doing, you may find it better to zoom in or out to see more or less of the worksheet at once. For example, to look at the worksheet as a whole, zoom out; to focus on particular cells, zoom in.

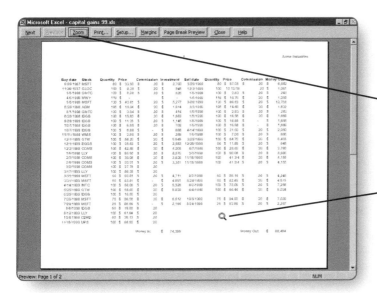

1. Click on the **Zoom button** to zoom to a closer view of your worksheet. The worksheet will be magnified.

Your mouse pointer is a magnifying glass while zoomed out in Print Preview. Position it over any area of the worksheet and click to zoom in on that area.

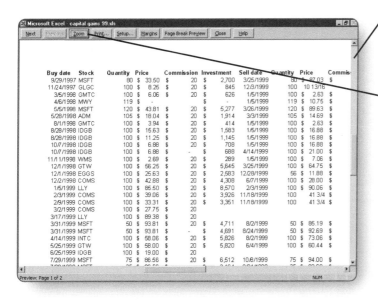

While zoomed in, you can use the scroll bars to view different parts of the worksheet.

2. Click on **Zoom** again. The worksheet will shrink.

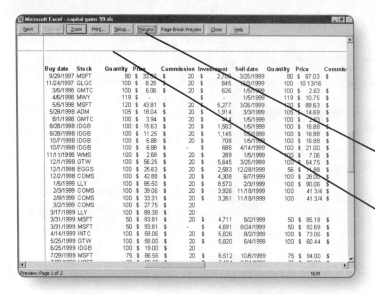

Adjusting Margins

The margin settings control where the worksheet will appear on the printed page. To adjust the margins, follow these steps.

1. Click on the **Margins button**.

The margin settings, columns, and header and footer areas of your worksheet will be revealed.

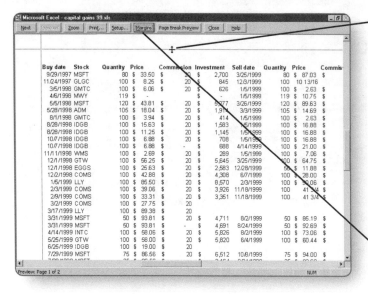

2. Move the **mouse pointer** over a margin line until it changes to a double-headed arrow.

3. Press and **hold** the **mouse button** as you drag the margin in or out, or up or down.

4. Release the **mouse button**. The new setting will take effect.

5. Click the **Margins button** again. The margin lines will be turned off.

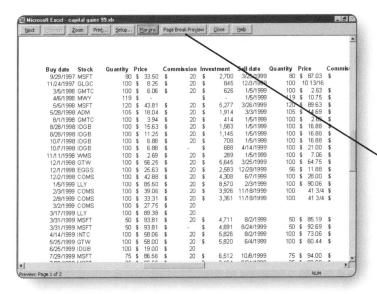

Previewing Page Breaks

Page breaks are inserted by Excel to divide large worksheets into pages.

1. Click on **Page Break Preview**. The Welcome to Page Break Preview dialog box will open.

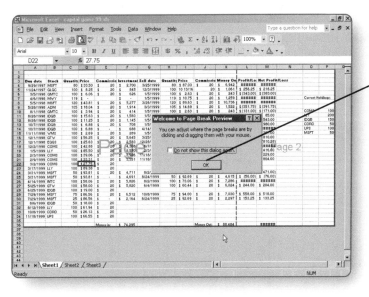

2. Click on **OK**. In the worksheet, you will see where Excel has inserted page breaks either because it knows it can't fit more information on a page or because you selected a particular page range. You can move page breaks, to get a better grouping of rows on pages.

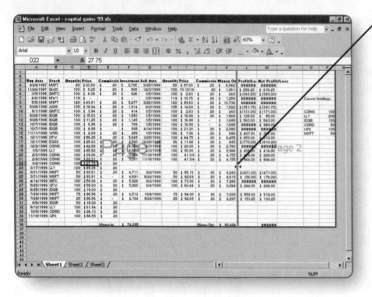

3. Point to a **page break line**. A double-headed arrow will appear.

4. Drag the **page break line** to a new position.

Closing Page Break Preview

When you are finished working with page breaks, return to Normal view with these steps.

1. Click on **View**. The View menu will appear.

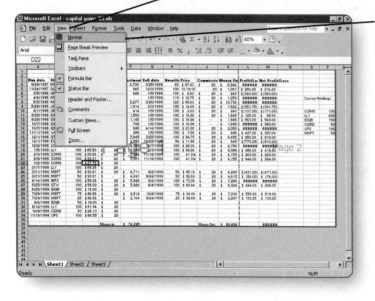

2. Click on **Normal**. You will return to Normal view.

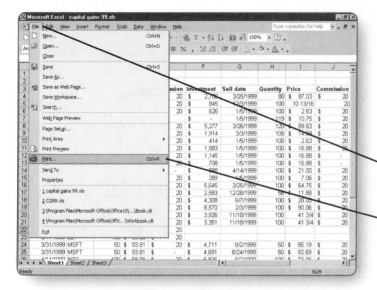

Printing Your Worksheet

Now that you've checked all your printing options, you are ready to print.

1. Click on **File**. The File menu will appear.

2. Click on **Print**. The Print dialog box will open.

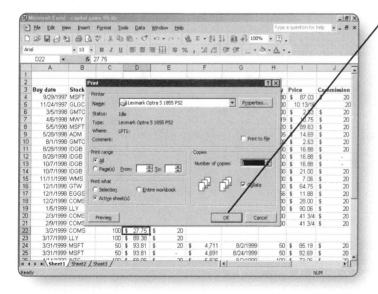

3. Click on **OK**. The document will be printed.

Refer to Chapter 3, "Saving, Printing, and Exiting Excel," for more information about options in the Print dialog box.

Part II Review Questions

1. In Excel, what is a range? *See "Selecting Cells" in Chapter 5*

2. How can you quickly fill a range with a series of data? *See "Filling a Range" in Chapter 5*

3. What role do formulas play in Excel? *See "Entering a Simple Calculation" in Chapter 6*

4. What are functions? *See "Using Built-In Functions" in Chapter 6*

5. Why would you want to name a range? *See "Naming a Range" in Chapter 7*

6. How can you sort the data rows in a particular order? *See "Sorting Data" in Chapter 8*

7. To create a template for default blank workbooks, what do you name it, and where do you store it? *See "Modifying the Default Workbook Settings" in Chapter 9*

8. What are Spreadsheet Solutions? *See "Creating a New Workbook with a Template" in Chapter 9*

9. What feature can you use to see your worksheet before you print it? *See "Previewing Your Worksheet" in Chapter 10*

10. What does Page Break Preview allow you to change? *See "Previewing Page Breaks" in Chapter 10*

PART III

Making Your Data Look Good

11

Formatting Text

You can make your worksheets easier to read and more interesting by formatting text effectively. You can use different fonts; change the alignment; add borders, lines, and colors; and more! In this chapter, you'll learn how to:

- Use AutoFormat
- Change the type and size of a font
- Use bold, italic, and underline styles
- Align your text
- Center a heading across your worksheet
- Copy text formatting

Using AutoFormat

If you're not artistically inclined, AutoFormat is a great tool for creating great-looking worksheets quickly and easily. AutoFormat allows you to choose from a number of professionally designed formats that automatically add colors, fonts, lines, borders, and more to your worksheets.

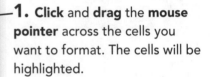

1. **Click** and **drag** the **mouse pointer** across the cells you want to format. The cells will be highlighted.

2. **Click** on **Format**. The Format menu will appear.

3. **Click** on **AutoFormat**. The AutoFormat dialog box will open.

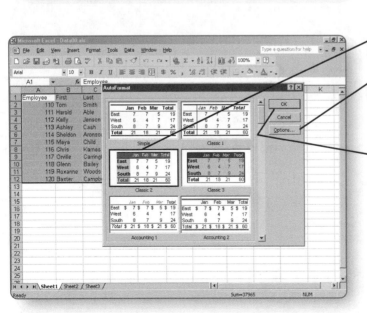

4. **Click** on a **sample format**.

You can set additional options by clicking on the Options button.

5. **Click** on **OK** when you find an effect you like. The effect will be applied to the selected cells.

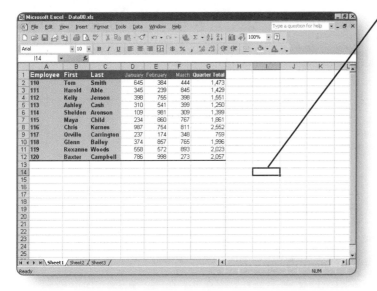

6. Click away from the cells. The cells will be deselected, and you will be able to see the full effect of the formatting.

Depending on your selection, AutoFormat may have applied color, changed your fonts, applied italic or bold, and adjusted row heights.

Removing AutoFormat

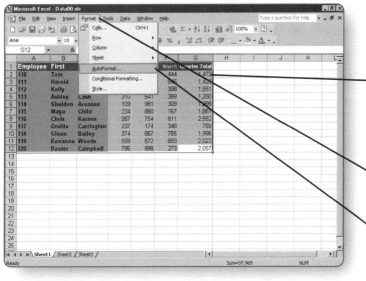

If you do not like the look that AutoFormat has provided, you can easily remove it.

1. Reselect the **cells** containing the AutoFormatting if they are not selected. The cells will be highlighted.

2. Click on **Format**. The Format menu will appear.

3. Click on **AutoFormat**. The AutoFormat dialog box will open.

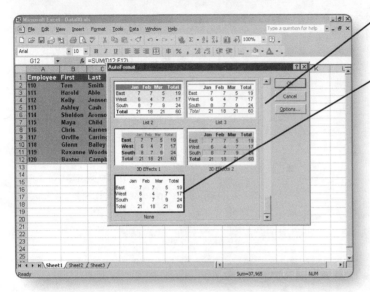

4. **Scroll** to the **bottom** of the AutoFormats.

5. **Click** on **None** from the list of formats. (It's all the way at the bottom of the list.) The selection will be highlighted.

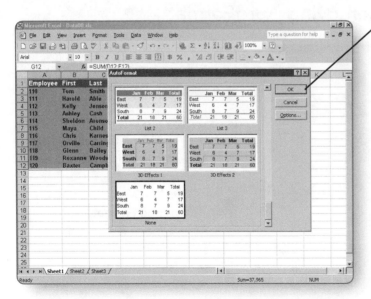

6. **Click** on **OK**. AutoFormat will be removed from your worksheet.

Using Fonts

Fonts are typefaces in different styles and sizes that give your text character and impact.

1. **Select** the **cell(s)** containing the text you want to format. The cell(s) will be highlighted.

2. **Click** on **Format**. The Format menu will appear.

3. **Click** on **Cells**. The Format Cells dialog box will open.

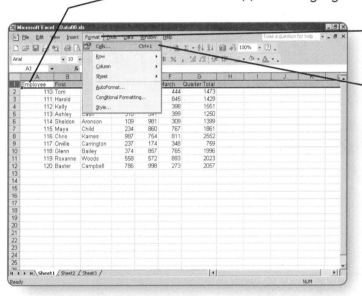

4. **Click** on the **Font tab**. In this tab, you can select:

- A Font, Font style, and Size from the drop-down lists

- Underline, Color, and Effects

As you make your selections, you can preview the results.

5. **Click** on **OK** when you're happy with the preview.

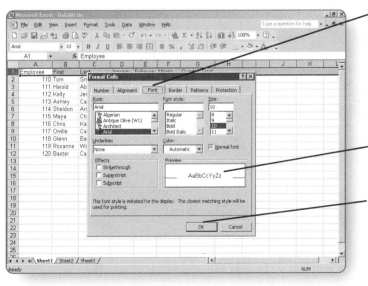

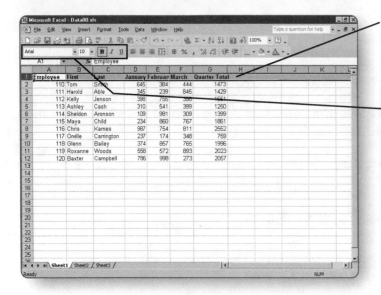

Your selections will be applied to the text.

NOTE

You can also change the font, font size, font color, and other attributes using the Formatting toolbar controls. Some of these are covered in the next section.

NOTE

After you change font size or apply an effect, the text might not fit in its column anymore. Refer back to Chapter 5 for help changing column width.

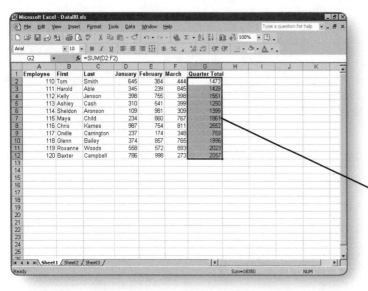

Adding Bold, Italic, and Underline

You can apply bold, italic, and underline formatting from the toolbar.

1. Click and **drag** the **mouse pointer** across the range of cells containing the text you want to format. The cells will be highlighted.

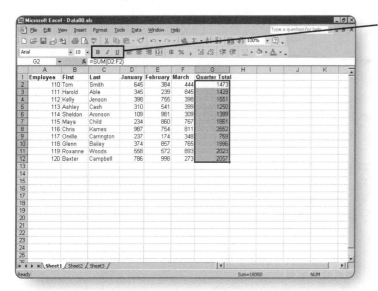

2. **Click** on the **Bold**, **Italic**, or **Underline buttons**. The effect(s) will be immediately applied to your text.

NOTE

You can apply more than one attribute to the selected text. Each of the attributes is an on/off toggle; to remove an effect, click its button again.

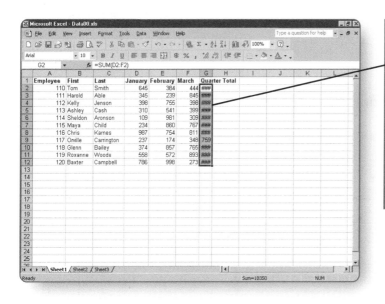

TIP

If the numbers become # symbols, the new font has made the text too wide to fit in the column. See Chapter 5, "Editing Worksheets," for information on adjusting column widths.

Aligning Your Text

You can make a worksheet easier to read by aligning the text appropriately. For example, you might want to center data beneath a heading or change the default alignment for text or numbers. (Text aligns to the left by default, and numbers to the right.)

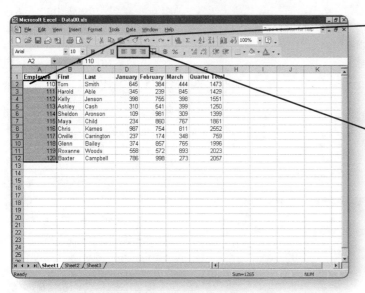

1. **Click** and **drag** the **mouse pointer** across the range of cells with the text that needs to be aligned. The cells will be highlighted.

2. **Click** on the **Left**, **Center**, or **Right align buttons**. The cell content will be aligned. In this example, the selected cells are right-aligned.

Centering a Heading Over More Than One Column

If you want to center a heading over more than one column, use the Merge and Center button.

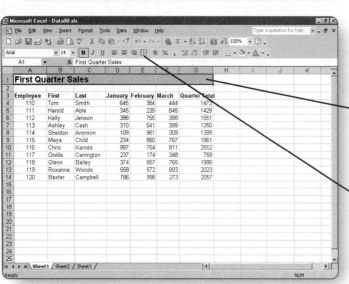

1. **Click** and **drag** the **mouse pointer** across the range of cells that need to have centered text. The cells will be highlighted.

2. **Click** on the **Merge and Center button**. The cells will be merged into one large cell and the content will be centered in it.

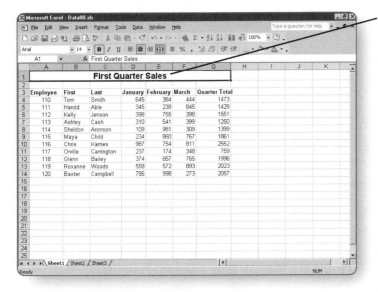

In this example, seven cells have been merged into one large cell, A1. The text has also been centered. When you merge several cells, the new larger cell uses the address of the rightmost cell in the range.

Other Alignment Options

You can also merge cells, wrap text in a cell, vertically align, shrink text to fit, and rotate text.

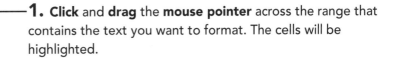

1. Click and **drag** the **mouse pointer** across the range that contains the text you want to format. The cells will be highlighted.

2. Click on **Format**. The Format menu will appear.

3. Click on **Cells**. The Format Cells dialog box will open.

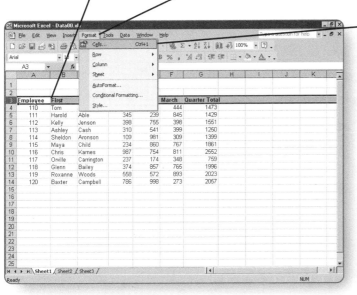

4. Click on the **Alignment tab**. The tab will come to the front.

5. Click on **whatever option** you want to select and change.

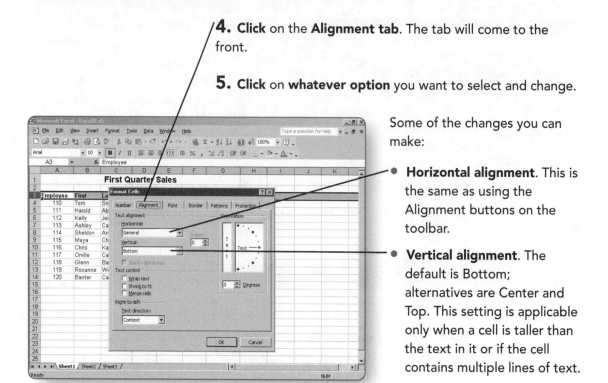

Some of the changes you can make:

- **Horizontal alignment**. This is the same as using the Alignment buttons on the toolbar.

- **Vertical alignment**. The default is Bottom; alternatives are Center and Top. This setting is applicable only when a cell is taller than the text in it or if the cell contains multiple lines of text.

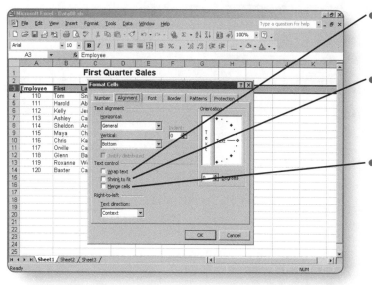

- **Wrap text**. Allows text in the cell to wrap to multiple lines if it does not fit horizontally.

- **Shrink to fit**. Decreases the font in the cell so that the text fits on a single line in that cell.

- **Merge cells**. Merges two or more selected cells into a single cell, as with the Merge and Center button from the preceding section.

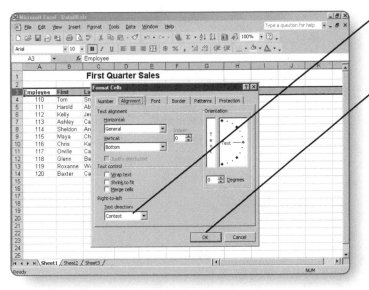

● **Text direction**. Sets text to run left to right or right to left in the cell.

6. Click on **OK**. The change(s) you made will be applied.

Copying Text Formatting

Excel includes the Format Painter feature, which copies formatting from one cell to another. It copies not only font size and text attributes but also any number formatting, borders, shading, and alignment that you might have set for the cell(s) being copied. (You will learn about number formatting, borders, and shading in Chapter 12.)

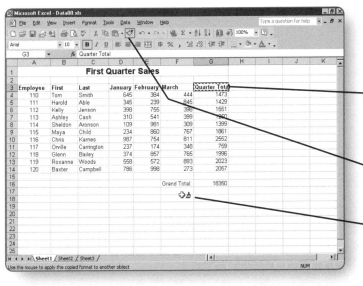

1. Select a **cell** that contains the formatting you want to copy.

2. Click on the **Format Painter button** on the toolbar.

The mouse pointer will turn into a paintbrush with a plus sign.

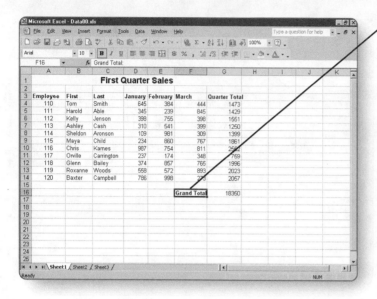

3a. **Click** on a **single cell** to receive the formatting.

OR

3b. **Drag** across the **range of cells** to receive the formatting. The cells will be "painted" with the formatting of the original cell.

12

Formatting Numbers and Cells

The numbers you enter in a worksheet represent many values, such as dollars and cents, percentages, and dates. You need to format your raw numbers so that they're easy to recognize. You can also draw attention to particular cells with color, shading, and borders. In this chapter, you'll learn how to:

- Add dollar signs and decimal places
- Format percentages
- Format dates
- Add cell borders
- Apply color backgrounds and patterns

Applying Number Formatting

Number formats enable you to quickly recognize numerical amounts in a worksheet, such as currency and percentages. Number formats also can specify a number of decimal places to show, display negative numbers in red or in parentheses, and more.

Formatting Currency

When you format text as currency, a currency symbol appears to its left (usually a $ sign, unless you have set up Excel for a foreign currency), and two decimal places appear in the number.

1. **Click** and **drag** the **mouse pointer** across the range that contains or will contain currency. The cells will be highlighted.

2. **Click** on the **Currency Style button**. The selection will be formatted.

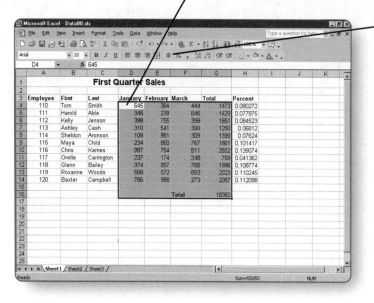

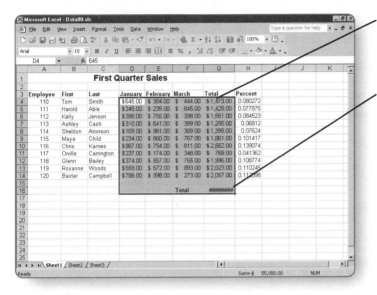

Excel will add a dollar sign, a decimal point, and cents to each entry in the selected range.

If # marks appear in a cell, widen the column, as you learned in Chapter 5, "Editing Worksheets."

Formatting Percentages

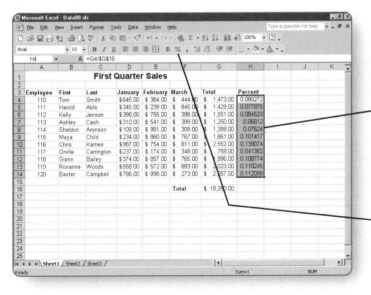

The procedure for formatting numbers to be displayed as percentages is almost exactly the same as for currency.

1. Click and **drag** the **mouse pointer** across the range containing the data that you want to format as percentages. The cells will be highlighted.

2. Click on the **Percent Style button**. The selection will be formatted.

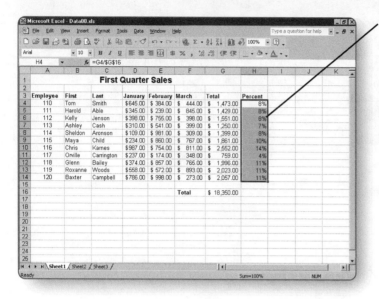

Percentages are much easier to read after they've been formatted. The numbers are rounded, and the percent sign added. Any decimal values not displayed are still used in all calculations.

Adding and Removing Decimal Places

Amounts formatted to currency have two decimal places added for the cents. Percentages are rounded to a whole number. In either case, you may want to hide or display numbers after the decimal point.

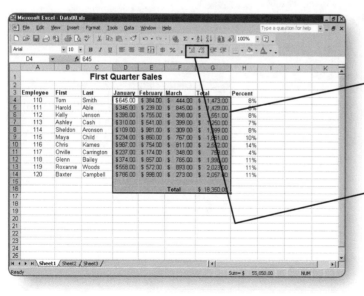

1. **Click** and **drag** the **mouse pointer** across the range of cells that contain the numbers you want to format. The cells will be highlighted.

2. **Click** on either the **Increase** or **Decrease Decimal buttons**. The decimal places will increase or decrease.

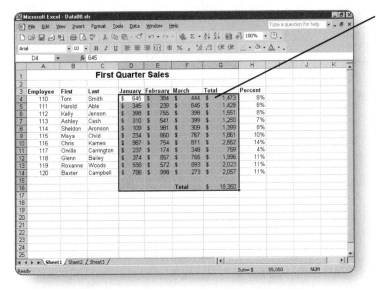

In this example, after clicking twice on the Decrease Decimal button, two decimal places have disappeared.

NOTE

Even if you display numbers with decimal values as whole numbers, the numbers after the decimal point will still be used in all calculations.

Formatting Dates

You can format any number as a date or time. When Excel displays a number in date format, it counts the number of days since January 1, 1900, and ignores any digits to the right of the decimal. For example, the number 1,000.25 would appear as 9/26/1902 when formatted as a date. When you format a number as a time, it ignores any digits to the *left* of the decimal place and converts the number to the *right* of the decimal to a time. For example, 1,000.25 would appear as 6:00 AM (which is 1/4 of the time between 12:00 AM and 11:59 PM).

When you enter a date into a cell, Excel formats it as DD-MMM-YY. You can change to a different date format with the following procedure.

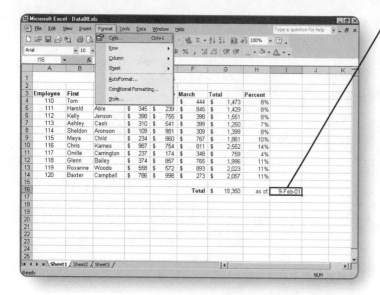

1. **Select** the **cell** or the **range** containing the date(s). The cell(s) will be highlighted.

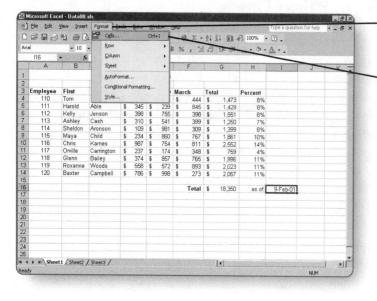

2. **Click** on **Format**. The Format menu will appear.

3. **Click** on **Cells**. The Format Cells dialog box will open.

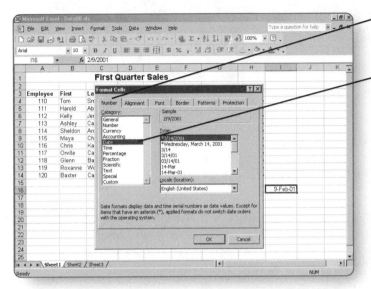

4. **Click** on the **Number tab**. The tab will come to the front.

5. **Click** on **Date** in the Category list. The item will be highlighted.

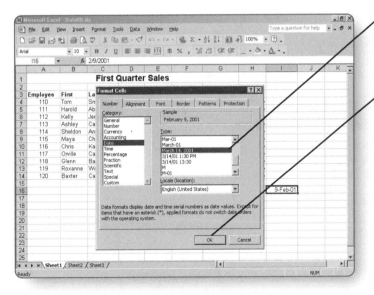

6. **Click** on a **format** in the Type list. A preview will appear in the Sample area.

7. **Click** on **OK**. The Format Cells dialog box will close.

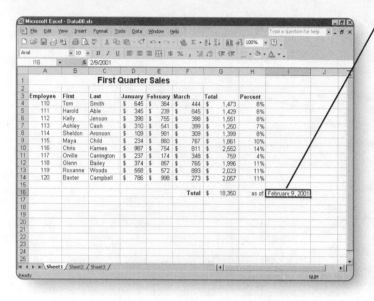

The new format for the date will appear in the cell.

As always, if # marks appear, widen the column, as you learned in Chapter 5.

NOTE

There are many other number formats to choose from, and many options for each one. Experiment with some of the other formats on the Number tab in the Format Cells dialog box when you have the time.

Applying Borders

You can add borders (lines) to individual cells and groups of cells. A border can appear around all sides, or only certain sides (for example, only the bottom of the selected area). A border should not be confused with an underline, which runs under individual text letters and can appear only beneath the text.

1. **Select** the **cell** or **range of cells** around which to put a border. The cell(s) will be highlighted.

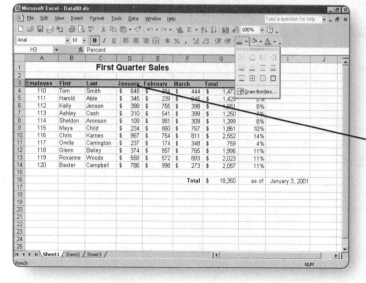

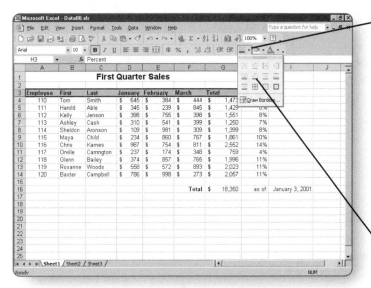

2. Click on the **down arrow** next to the Borders button. The Borders palette will appear.

Icons displaying how the borders will be applied to a cell or selected range (top, bottom, left, right, or a combination) and the weight of the line (thin, thick, or double) are displayed in the palette.

3. Click on your **selection**. The Borders palette will close.

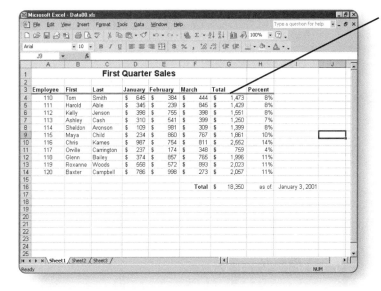

When you deselect the cell or range, you will see the border that you added.

Applying Colors and Patterns

If you have a color printer or you want to improve the look of your worksheet on your computer screen, you can add background colors. If you use a black-and-white printer, you can add shades of gray and patterns instead.

Adding a Background Color

Adding a background color can dress up a worksheet by making it more interesting-looking. Be careful, however, that the background you choose does not interfere with the readability of your data.

1. Select the **cell** or **range of cells** you want to color. The cells will be highlighted.

2. Click on **Format**. The Format menu will appear.

3. Click on **Cells**. The Format Cells dialog box will open.

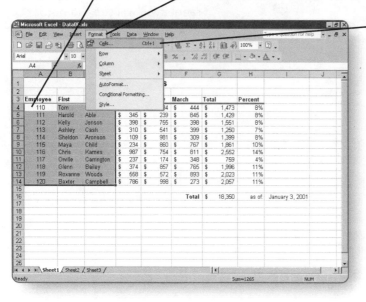

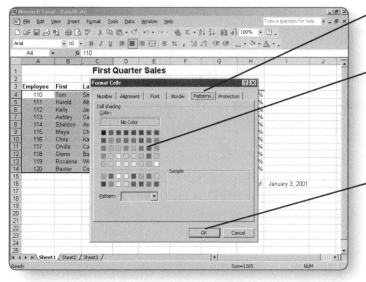

4. Click on the **Patterns tab**. The tab will come to the front.

5. Click on a **color** under the Color heading. The color box will be highlighted, and a preview will appear in the Sample box.

6. Click on **OK**. The color will be applied to the highlighted cells.

Adding a Pattern

You can use a pattern instead of a color as a background to your cells. A pattern uses two colors, arranged in some design, such as stripes or dots. Each pattern has both a background and a foreground color. The background color is the "base" color, whereas the foreground color is the color of the stripes or dots.

CAUTION

A pattern can impair the readability of the data in a cell. Use patterns sparingly, and keep them subtle.

1. Select the **cell** or **range of cells**. The cells will be highlighted.

2. Click on **Format**. The Format menu will appear.

3. Click on **Cells**. The Format Cells dialog box will open.

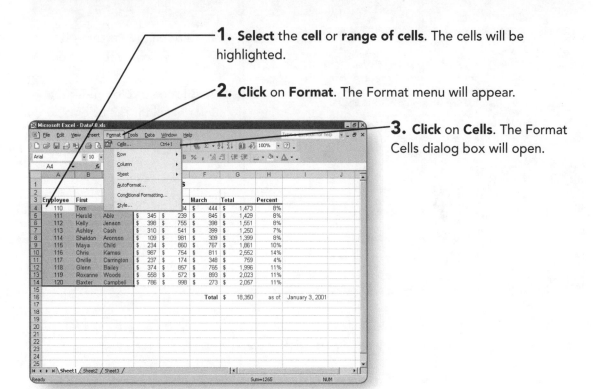

4. Click on the **Patterns tab**. The tab will come to the front.

5. Click on the **down arrow** next to Pattern to open the Pattern drop-down list. A palette of patterns and colors will appear.

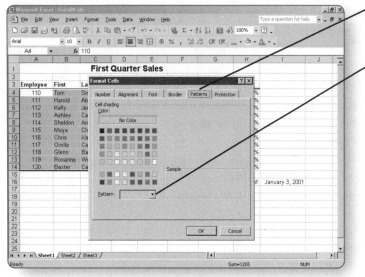

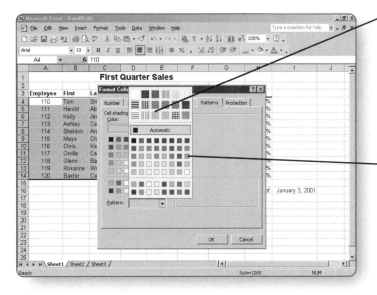

6. Click on a **pattern** at the top of the list. The drop-down list will close.

7. Click on the **down arrow** next to Pattern again. The drop-down list will appear.

8. Click on a **foreground color** to use. The list will close again.

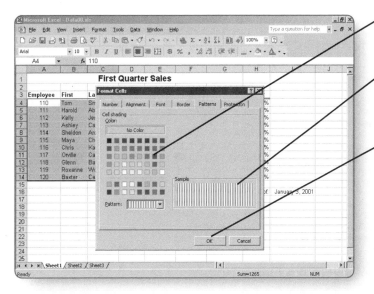

9. Click on a **background color** to use with this pattern.

10. Check your **work** in the Sample area, and repeat steps 5 through 9 as needed.

11. Click on **OK**. The Format Cells dialog box will close. Your changes will appear in the worksheet.

TIP

Remember that the pattern is a background, and if you will be entering data into the cells in the selected range, you need to select a light pattern, so that the data can still be read.

Part III Review Questions

1. Why would you want to use the AutoFormat feature? *See "Using AutoFormat" in Chapter 11*

2. Why does Excel sometimes replace your entries with # signs when you change some formatting, and what can you do about it? *See "Adding Bold, Italic, and Underline" in Chapter 11*

3. How can you center a heading over more than one column evenly? *See "Centering a Heading Over More Than One Column" in Chapter 11*

4. What's an easy way to copy formatting from one cell to another? *See "Copying Text Formatting" in Chapter 11*

5. Why do you need to format numbers? *See the introduction to Chapter 12*

6. How can you quickly format numbers in a cell as dollars and cents? *See "Formatting Currency" in Chapter 12*

7. What do the Increase Decimal and Decrease Decimal buttons do? *See "Adding and Removing Decimal Places" in Chapter 12*

8. How can you add the current date to your worksheet? *See "Formatting Dates" in Chapter 12*

9. What's the difference between an underline and a border? *See "Applying Borders" in Chapter 12*

10. Why should you be careful when choosing patterns to apply to a cell? *See "Adding a Pattern" in Chapter 12*

PART IV

Adding Pictures and Charts

13

Adding Clip Art and WordArt to a Worksheet

Whether you need to make a presentation of financial information to the Board of Directors or PTA, you can add interest and flair to your document with pictures and WordArt. In this chapter, you'll learn how to:

- Add clip art and adjust its size and placement
- Adjust the contrast and brightness of clip art
- Insert a picture from a file
- Add and edit WordArt

Adding Clip Art

Clip art is a graphic or drawing file that has been created for you to use. By using clip art, you can quickly and easily add illustrations to your document. You choose clip art from the Microsoft Clip Organizer.

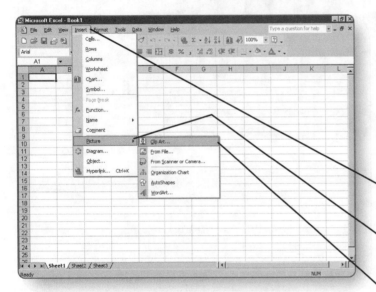

Opening the Clip Art Controls

The clip art controls in Office XP are different from earlier versions. They appear in the task pane to the right of the work area.

1. **Click** on **Insert**. The Insert menu will appear.

2. **Click** on **Picture**. A submenu will appear.

3. **Click** on **Clip Art**.

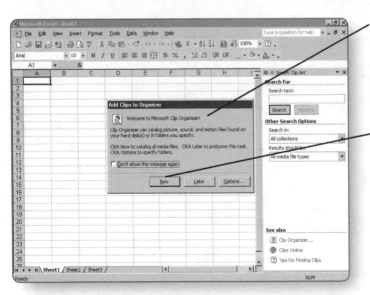

If this is the first time you have used the Clip Organizer, a box will appear asking whether you want to catalog the available clips.

4. **Click Now** and wait for the cataloging to take place. It takes only a minute or two.

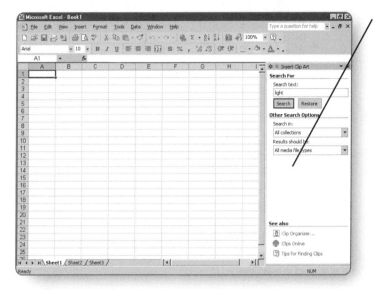

When the cataloging is complete, the Insert Clip Art controls appear in the task pane.

Searching for a Clip Art Image

The Insert Clip Art task pane provides controls for searching for a clip by keyword. Each clip has at least one keyword that describes it; you can type a word to search for and retrieve images that match your specification.

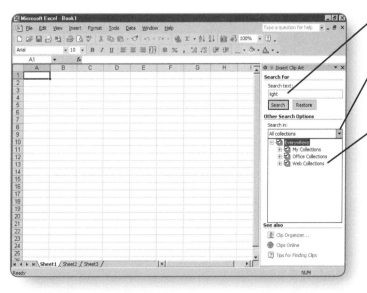

1. **Type** a **search word** in the Search text box.

2. **Click** the **down arrow** next to Search in.

3. **Deselect** any **collections** you don't want to include.

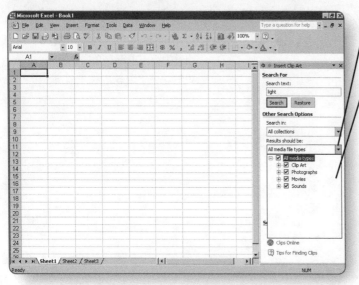

4. Click the **down arrow** next to Results should be.

5. Deselect any **media clip types** you don't want to include in the results.

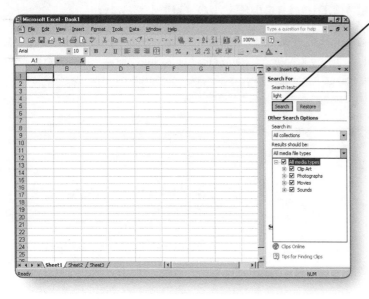

6. Click on **Search**. Clips matching the keyword and specifications you entered will appear.

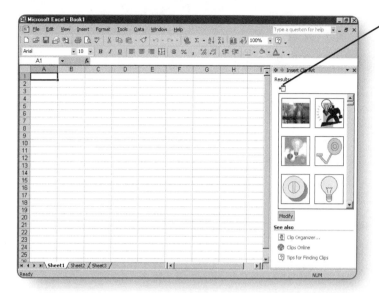

7. (Optional) **Click** on the **Expand Results** button. A larger window of found clips will appear.

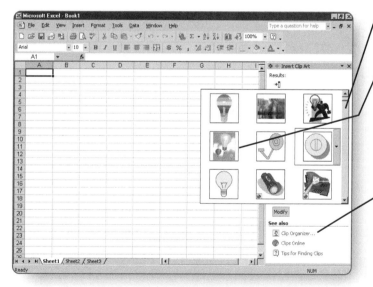

8. Scroll through the **list** to find a picture.

9. Double-click on the **clip** you want. It will be placed on the worksheet.

NOTE

Another way to locate a clip is to browse by category. To do so, click on Clip Organizer and select from a category in any available clip collection, including clip collections on the Internet.

Selection handles will be visible around the clip.

The picture toolbar will also open.

10. Click on **Close**. The Insert Clip Art task pane will close.

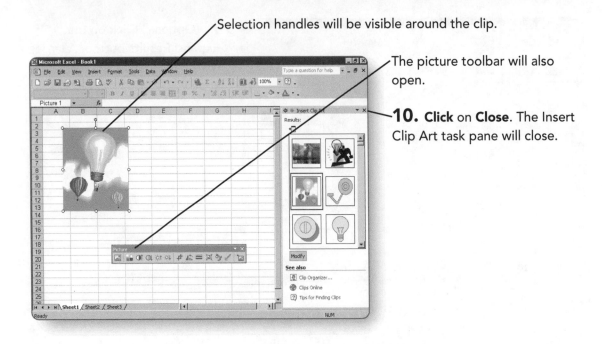

Adjusting the Size and Location of Clip Art

Clip art floats above the worksheet itself, in a separate layer. When you first insert a clip, it is rather large and probably obscures some of your data. You will want to size and position the graphic so it accentuates your overall presentation, rather than interferes with it.

Adjusting the Size of Clip Art

The clip art that comes with Office may not be exactly the size you need for a particular spot. You can easily resize any piece to fit your needs.

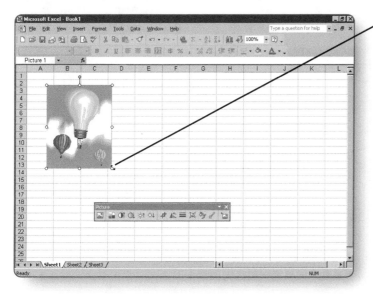

1. **Move** the **mouse pointer** over one of the selection handles. The arrow will change to a double-headed arrow.

2. **Press** and **hold** the **mouse button** until the pointer changes to a crosshair.

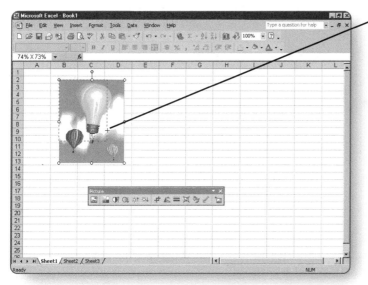

3. **Drag** the **selection handle** in or out. A dotted outline will show where it is going.

4. **Release** the **mouse button**. The picture will shrink or expand, depending on which way you drag.

NOTE

Dragging a corner selection handle sizes a clip art image proportionally. Dragging a top or side handle increases the width or height only, distorting the image.

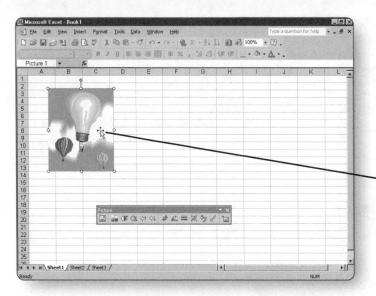

Moving the Clip Art Image

After you have placed a piece of clip art and resized it as needed, you may want to reposition it on the page.

1. Move the **mouse pointer** over the picture. The mouse pointer will change to a white arrow with a four-headed black arrow attached.

2. Press and **hold** the **mouse button** and **drag** the **picture** to a new location. A dotted outline will show where the picture is going.

3. Release the **mouse button**. The clip art will be moved.

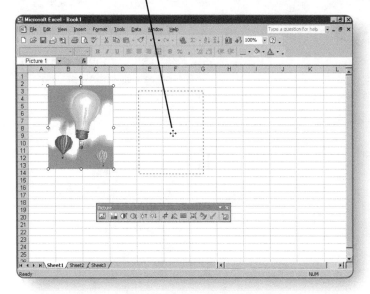

TIP

When you finally decide where the clip art image looks best, you may find you need to move your data so that it isn't obscured. This is easy. You can use the Cut and Paste commands covered in Chapter 5, "Editing Worksheets," or you can insert some blank columns or rows (see Chapter 4, "Managing Workbooks and Worksheets").

Adjusting the Quality of the Picture

Using the Picture toolbar, you can make adjustments to the picture after you've inserted it.

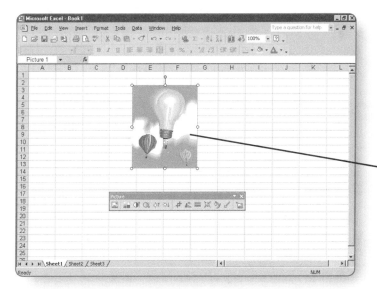

NOTE

If the Picture toolbar does not appear, open the View menu, point to Toolbars, and click on Picture.

1. **Click** on the **clip art** or other picture that you have inserted. The selection handles will appear, as well as the Picture toolbar.

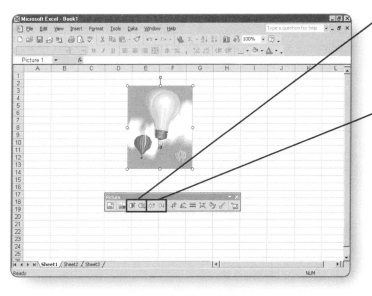

2. **Click** on the **More Contrast** or **Less Contrast button**. The contrast in the picture will increase or decrease.

3. **Click** on the **More Brightness** or **Less Brightness button**. The brightness in the picture will increase or decrease.

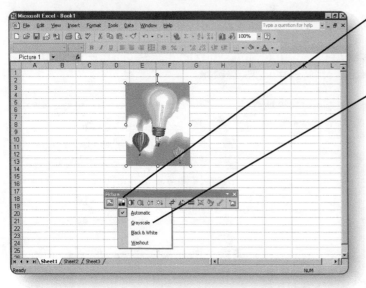

4. Click on the **Image Control button**. A list of image types will appear.

5. Click on the **image type** you want.

If you are not sure, try each type in turn. Automatic is color; Grayscale is a shaded black-and-white version. Black & White contains no shading. Washout is a pale ghost of the color image.

Inserting a Picture from a File

In addition to using the clip art provided with Excel, you may want to insert your own pictures that you have scanned or acquired elsewhere.

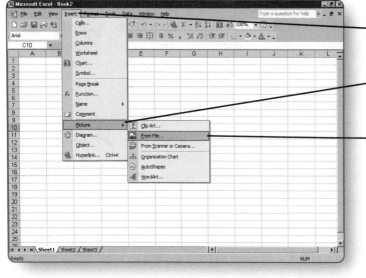

1. Click on **Insert**. The Insert menu will appear.

2. Click on **Picture**. A submenu will appear.

3. Click on **From File**. The Insert Picture dialog box will open.

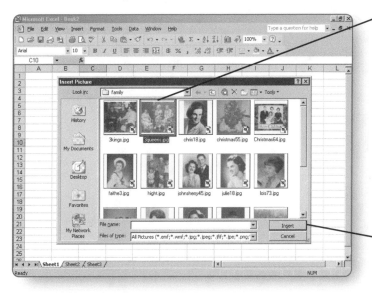

4. Click on the **picture** you want to insert. It will be selected.

NOTE

You may need to change the folder using the Look in drop-down list. Refer back to Chapter 4 if you need help with this.

5. Click on **Insert**. The picture will be inserted in your worksheet.

NOTE

After you insert the picture, you can resize and move it just like you did with the clip art earlier in the chapter.

Cropping an Image

Excel provides a cropping tool that lets you trim extraneous detail from one or more sides of a picture. This works with both clip art and other images.

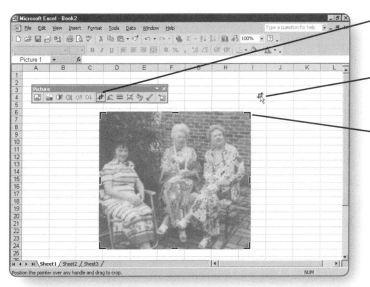

1. Click on the **Crop button** on the Picture toolbar.

The mouse pointer will change to the cropping tool.

2. Point the **mouse** at a selection handle in a corner that you want to crop out.

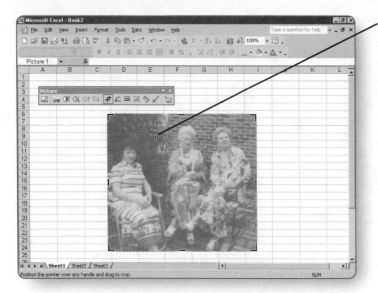

3. **Press** and **hold** the **mouse button** and drag the crosshair in toward the center of the picture. A dotted line will show where it is cropping.

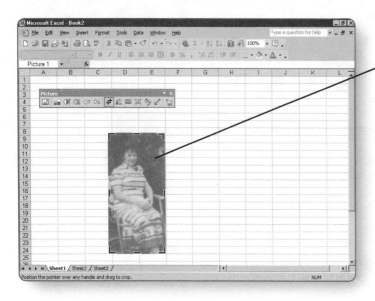

4. **Release** the **mouse button**.

The clip art will be adjusted to the new size.

5. **Repeat steps 2 through 4**, dragging different selection handles around the image, until it is cropped to your satisfaction.

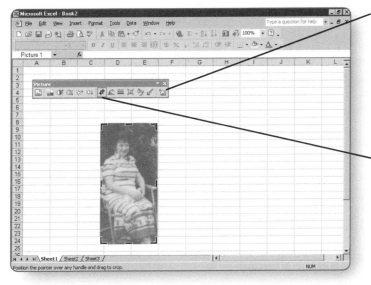

If you crop too much, click on the Reset Picture button, and the cropping will be removed. This button also returns color, brightness, and contrast changes to their original settings.

6. Click on the **Crop button** again. The cropping tool will be deselected.

Adding WordArt

Fonts can add some interest to your text, but for a more dramatic effect, try using WordArt. You can apply amazing color schemes, add three-dimensional effects, and sculpt your words into various shapes. With WordArt, the characters in the words form the artwork.

1. Click on **Insert**. The Insert menu will appear.

2. Click on **Picture**. A submenu will appear.

3. Click on **WordArt**. The WordArt Gallery dialog box will open.

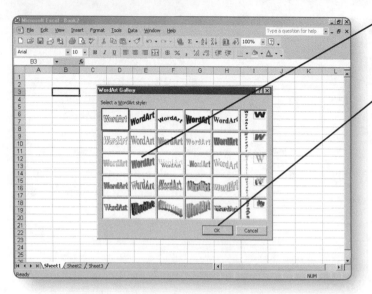

4. Click on a **style** in the WordArt Gallery. A border will appear around your selection.

5. Click on **OK**. The Edit WordArt Text dialog box will open.

6. Type in **text** to replace "Your Text Here."

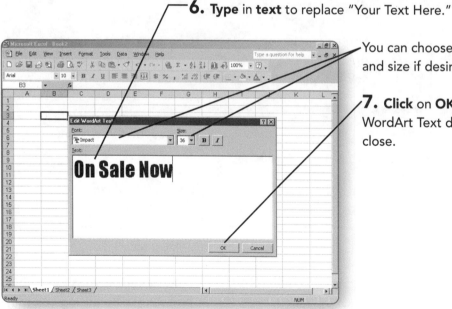

You can choose a different font and size if desired.

7. Click on **OK**. The Edit WordArt Text dialog box will close.

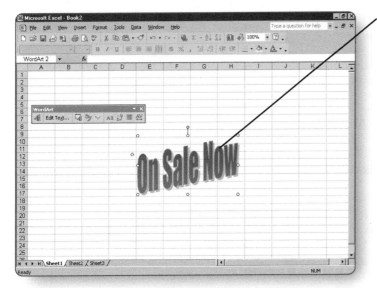

The text will appear in a layer above your worksheet surrounded by selection handles.

Changing the Look of Your WordArt

You can move and resize WordArt just as you learned to do with clip art earlier in the chapter. You can also make many adjustments to WordArt from the WordArt toolbar.

Rotating WordArt

Part of the fun of WordArt is that it isn't limited to straight horizontal orientation. You can rotate it a little—or a lot.

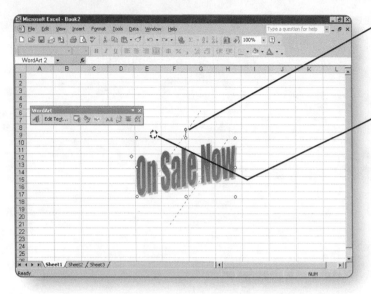

1. Point at the **green circle** at the top of the WordArt. The mouse pointer will turn into a circular arrow.

2. Hold down the **mouse button** and **drag**. The WordArt will rotate in the direction you drag.

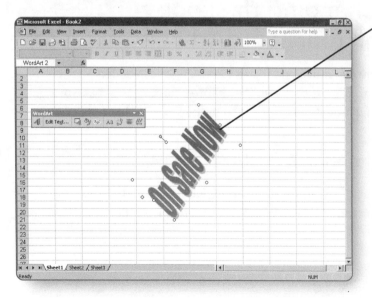

3. Release the **mouse button**. The WordArt will appear rotated.

Changing the WordArt Shape

The shape of the WordArt is the curve, line, or solid shape to which it conforms. Each WordArt style has a default shape, but you can change it easily.

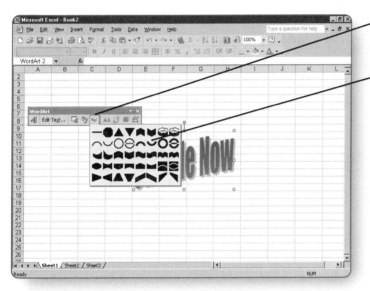

1. **Click** on the **WordArt Shape button**. A palette will appear.

2. **Click** on a **different shape** for the letters to follow. The WordArt changes to conform to the new shape.

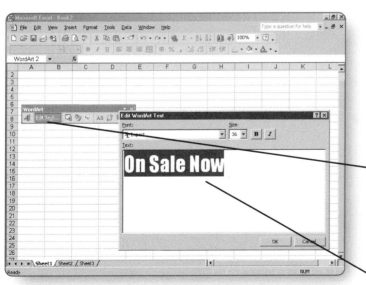

Editing WordArt Text

If you want to change the WordArt text, you do not have to re-create it; simply edit the text as described here.

1. **Click** on the **Edit Text button** to correct typing errors or make changes to the text. The Edit WordArt Text dialog box will open.

2. **Make** your **changes**.

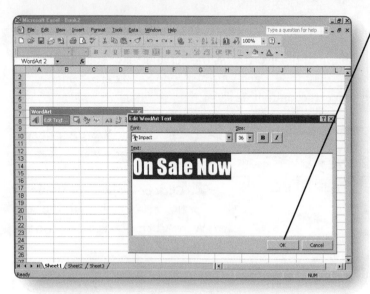

3. Click on **OK**. Your changes will appear in the document.

TIP

There is more that you can do with WordArt editing! Try out the four buttons on the right end of the WordArt toolbar, which control the way the text is sized, aligned, and spaced. You can also drag the yellow diamond(s) on the WordArt to change the perspective. Use Ctrl+Z to undo if you make a mistake.

14

Generating
a Chart

If you've ever spent hours creating charts on graph paper, you'll really appreciate how easy creating a chart is in Excel. Just make a few choices, and you will see your data transformed into a three-dimensional pie chart complete with data labels. In this chapter, you'll learn how to:

- Use the Chart Wizard to create a chart
- Change the chart type
- Change the way the data is plotted

Creating a Chart with the Chart Wizard

The Chart Wizard is really amazing. It enables you to create a sophisticated chart of your data in just a few minutes.

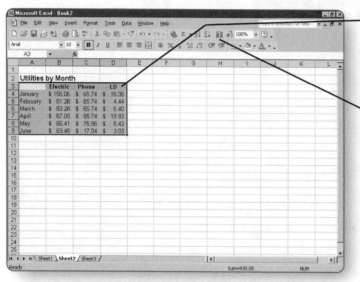

1. **Click** and **drag** the **mouse pointer** across the range that you want to chart. The cells will be highlighted.

2. **Click** on the **Chart Wizard button**. The Chart Wizard – Step 1 of 4 dialog box will open.

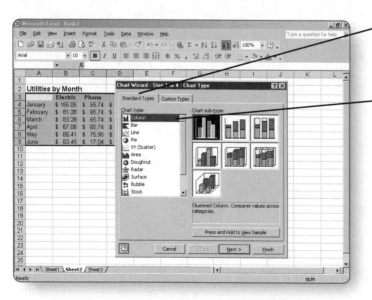

3. **Click** on the **Standard Types tab**. The tab will come to the front if it is not already there.

4. **Click** on a **chart type**. The item will be highlighted.

> **TIP**
>
> You can choose any chart type, but if you have more than one data series (that is, multiple rows and multiple columns in your range), don't choose Pie. Pie charts plot only a single row or a single column of figures.

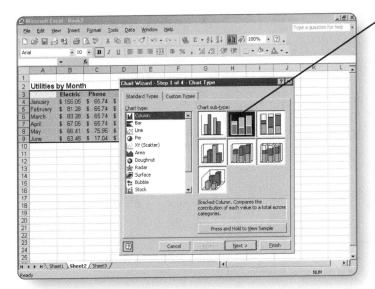

5. **Click** on an **option** in the Chart sub-type area. The item will be highlighted.

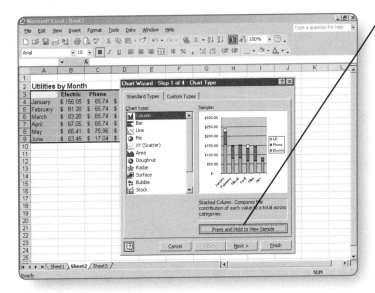

6. **Click** and **hold** down the **mouse button** on the Press and Hold to View Sample button. You will be able to see what your data will look like if you choose a particular chart type. Release the mouse button when you're finished looking.

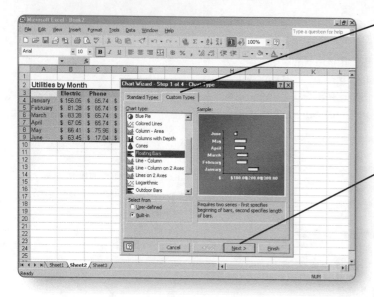

(Optional) As an alternative to selecting a standard chart type, you can also click on the Custom Types tab. You can choose from charts that have the background, colors, and fonts preselected.

7. Click on **Next** after choosing either a standard or custom chart type. The Chart Wizard – Step 2 of 4 dialog box will open.

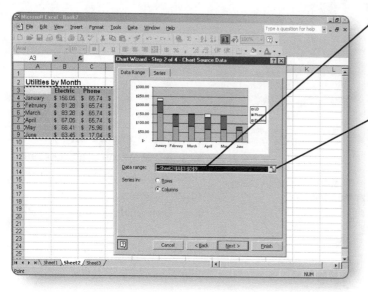

If you selected your data before clicking on the Chart Wizard in step 2, the data will appear in the Data range box.

You can change the data by typing a new range or by clicking on the Collapse Dialog button for the dialog box. Select the range in the worksheet, and then click on the Expand Dialog button for the dialog box to return to the wizard.

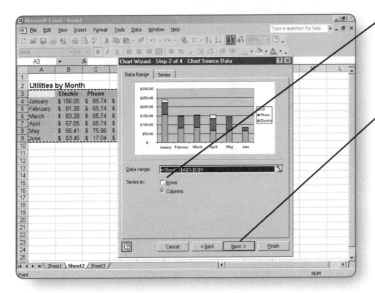

8. **Click** on **Rows** or **Columns**. See the sample to determine which way best conveys your message.

9. **Click** on **Next**. The Chart Wizard – Step 3 of 4 dialog box will open.

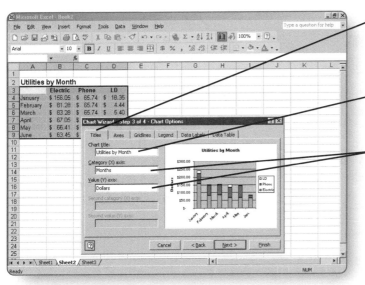

10. **Click** on the **Titles tab**. The tab will come to the front if it is not already there.

11. **Type** a **title** for your chart in the Chart title text box.

12. (Optional) **Type titles** for the X and/or Y axes if you think it will be helpful.

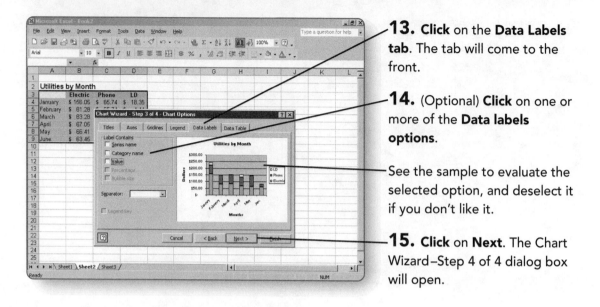

13. **Click** on the **Data Labels tab**. The tab will come to the front.

14. (Optional) **Click** on one or more of the **Data labels options**.

See the sample to evaluate the selected option, and deselect it if you don't like it.

15. **Click** on **Next**. The Chart Wizard–Step 4 of 4 dialog box will open.

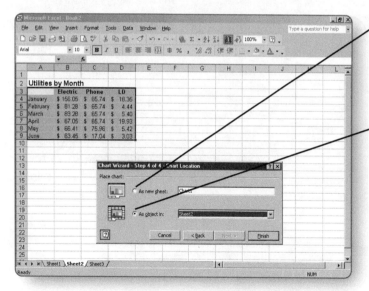

16a. **Click** on **As new sheet** to create your chart on a new worksheet.

OR

16b. **Click** on **As object in** to add it to the worksheet that contains the data, so that you can print both the data and the chart on the same page.

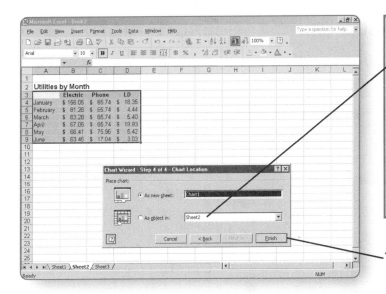

NOTE

By default, the sheet from which the data is taken appears in the As object in box. You can open this drop-down list and choose a different existing sheet in the workbook for the chart position if you want.

17. **Click** on **Finish**.

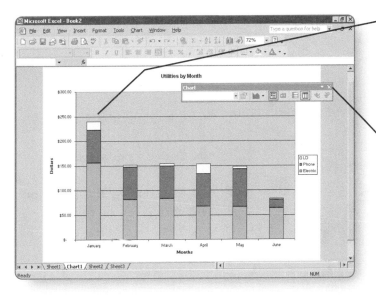

The chart will appear either in the current worksheet or in a new worksheet called Chart1, depending on your selection in step 16.

The Chart toolbar will also open.

Changing the Chart Type

You can change to a different chart type at any time, without re-creating the chart.

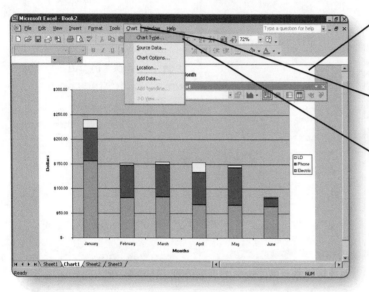

1. Click on the **chart** you want to work with. The chart will be selected.

2. Click on **Chart**. The Chart menu will appear.

3. Click on **Chart Type**. The Chart Type dialog box will open.

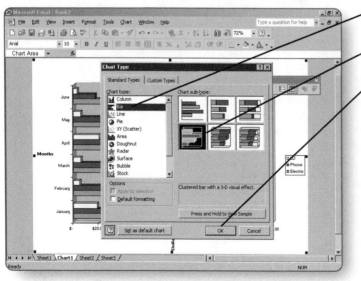

4. Click on a **new chart type**.

5. Click on a **new sub-type**.

6. Click on **OK**. The chart type will change for the selected chart.

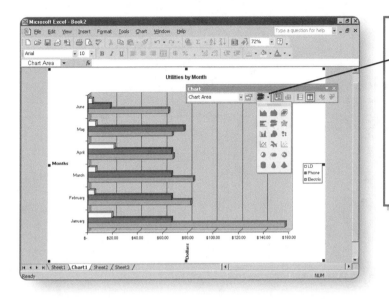

TIP

Another way to change chart types is to click the down arrow next to the Chart Type button on the Chart toolbar. A list of common chart types pops up; click on the one you want.

Changing How the Data Is Plotted

In the example charts you have seen so far in this chapter, each different color bar represents a different utility bill. This invites the reader to compare the cost of one utility bill versus another.

Alternatively, you could plot the same data so that each bar color represents a month. This would invite the reader to compare the utility costs month-by-month.

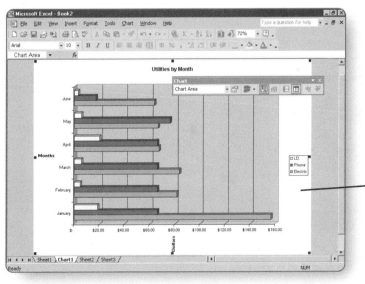

1. Click on the **chart** you want to work with. The chart will be selected.

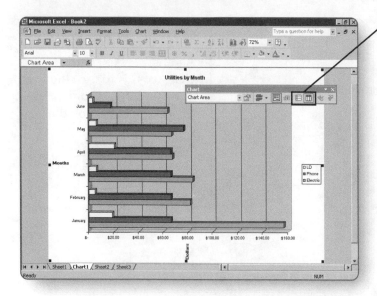

2. Click on the **By Column** or **By Row button** on the Chart toolbar. The way the data is plotted will change.

NOTE

If the Chart toolbar does not appear and you need to use it, choose View, Toolbars, Chart from the Excel menu.

Changing Which Cells Are Plotted

You can also change the range of cells on which the chart is based.

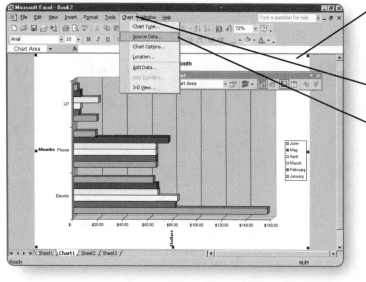

1. Click on the **chart** you want to work with. The chart will be selected.

2. Click on **Chart**.

3. Click on **Source Data**. The Source Data dialog box will open.

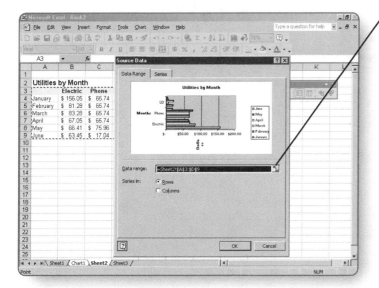

4. Click on the **Collapse Dialog button**. The dialog box will shrink to a title bar and a single line.

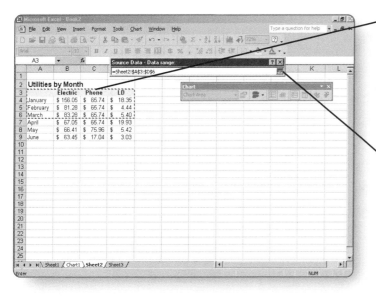

5. Drag across the **cells** you want to use. You might, for example, exclude a certain month or salesperson that you previously included. The cells will be highlighted.

6. Click on the **Expand Dialog button**. The dialog box will reopen.

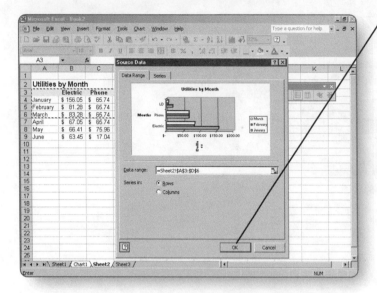

7. Click on **OK**. The chart will show the new range.

15

Formatting Your Chart

Excel has many formatting capabilities that can make your chart look even better. In this chapter, you'll learn how to:

- Improve label readability
- Add a legend
- Format individual parts of a chart

Making Labels Easier to Read

Although the wizard formats the chart, you may need to make some changes to improve its readability.

Changing Label Size and Color

Labels on a chart are often too small at their default size. You may want to make them larger and dress them up with some color.

1. **Click** on the **title label**. A box with selection handles will appear around it.

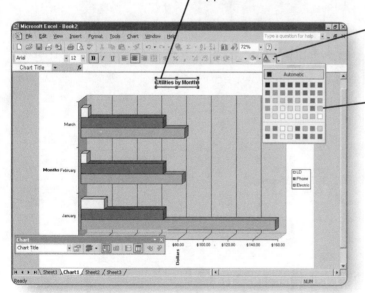

2. **Click** on the **down arrow** next to the Font Color button. The color palette will open.

3. **Click** on a **color** that will be more visible against the background color in your chart. The new color will appear on the title.

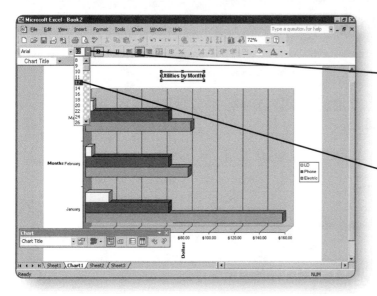

If the text is still a little small, you can change the font size.

4. Click on the **down arrow** next to the Font Size button, while the title is still selected. A drop-down list will appear.

5. Click on a **larger size**. The title will appear in the new size.

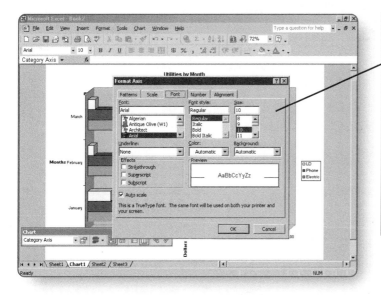

TIP

To change the font or font size for the axis labels (for example, January, February, March in this chart), double-click on the axis to open the Format Axis dialog box. On the Font tab, choose a larger font size, and then click OK.

Rotating Label Text

Some labels, especially labels along the vertical (Y) axis, may look better rotated 90 degrees.

1. Click on the **label** to rotate. A box with selection handles will appear around it.

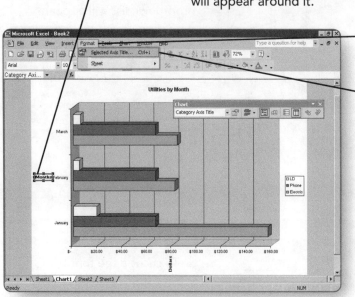

2. Click on **Format**. The Format menu will appear.

3. Click on **Selected Axis Title**. The Format Axis Title dialog box will open.

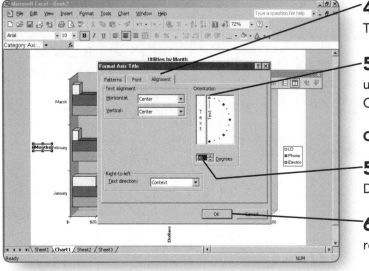

4. Click on the **Alignment tab**. The tab will come to the front.

5a. Drag the **red diamond** up to the top of the Orientation box.

OR

5b. Type 90 in the Degrees box.

6. Click on **OK**. The label will rotate.

When you place a vertical axis label parallel to a chart, there is more room for the chart, and the chart expands to fill the available space. Adjusting label rotation and positioning is one way to make a chart appear bigger without allocating more space on a worksheet for it.

If you want to rotate a particular label by 45 degrees up or down, you can use the Angle Text Downward and Angle Text Upward buttons on the Chart toolbar.

Adding Data Labels

On most bar and column charts, it's easy to find the value of a particular bar. Just follow its top to the value axis and read the number there. However, in some chart types, such as pie and scatter, it is not so easy to identify a value. In such cases, data labels can help.

1. Click on the **chart**. The chart will be selected.

2. Click on **Chart**. The Chart menu will appear.

3. Click on **Chart Options**. The Chart Options dialog box will open.

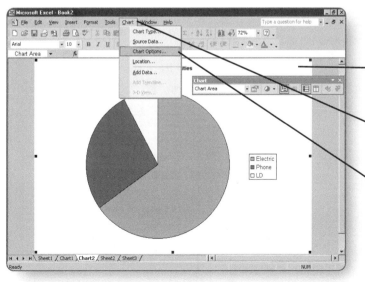

4. **Click** on the **Data Labels tab**. It will come to the front if it is not already there.

5. **Click** on a **data label type**. Percentage is good for pie charts; Value works well for many other types.

6. **Click** on **OK**. The chart will appear with the labels in place.

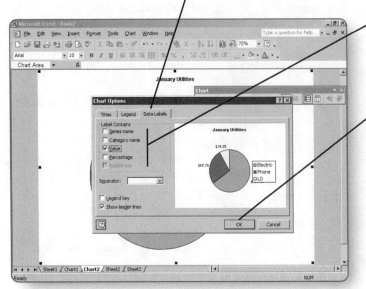

TIP

If you use Series Name or Category Name labels, the legend becomes redundant. You can turn it off using the steps in "Displaying or Hiding the Legend" later in this chapter.

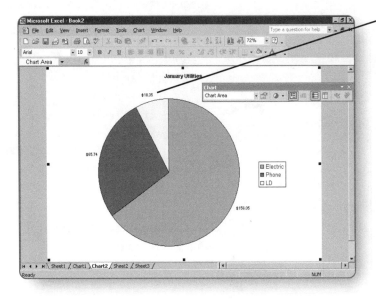

If the data labels are too small, as they are here, you can easily resize them. Just click on one of them (which selects them all), and then choose a different font size from the Font Size drop-down list.

TIP

The labels appear outside the pie slices by default, but you can move them on top of the slices if you prefer. See the following section to learn how to move labels.

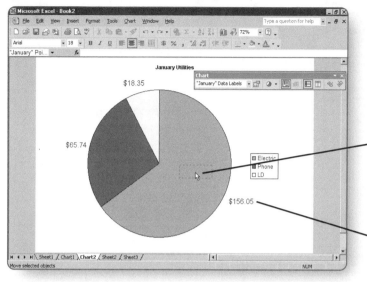

Moving Labels

Labels each appear in their own floating box, and you can drag those boxes anywhere on the chart.

1. Click on the **label** you want to move. A box with selection handles will appear around the label.

2. Click on the **border** of the label box and **drag it** to a new location. The box will be moved.

Resizing the Legend

The *legend* is the key that tells what each color or pattern represents. By default, it may be very small; follow these steps to make it larger.

1. Click on the **legend**. Click on the outer box of the legend rather than on an individual label within it. The legend will be selected.

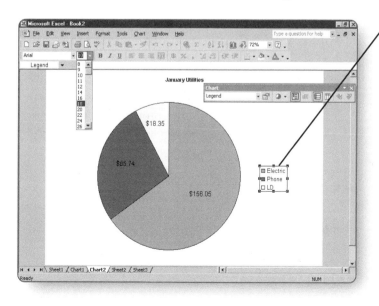

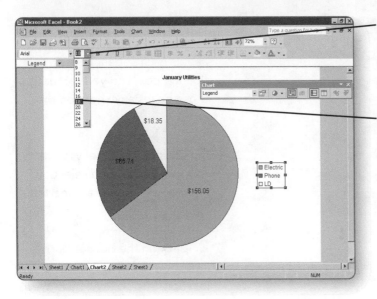

2. **Click** on the **down arrow** next to the Font Size control on the toolbar. The Font Size drop-down list will open.

3. **Click** on a **larger number**, such as 18. The size of the text in the legend will increase.

Displaying or Hiding the Legend

If you add data labels to a chart, the legend may become unnecessary. If so, you can hide it. Do not hide the legend, however, if it is needed to help the reader understand the chart.

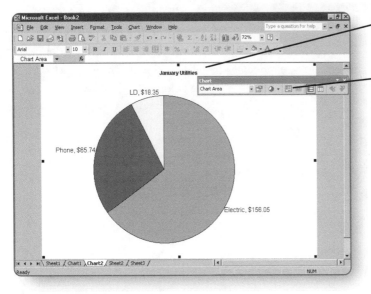

1. **Click** on the **chart** to select it. The Chart toolbar will appear.

2. **Click** on the **Legend button** on the Chart toolbar to toggle between showing and hiding the legend.

Displaying or Hiding a Data Table

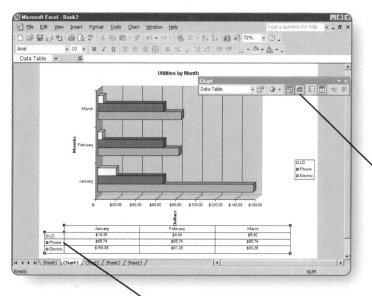

If the chart is on the same sheet as your data, a data table is redundant. However, if the chart is on a separate sheet, a data table can help the reader by providing the data on which the chart was based.

1. **Click** on the **Data Table button** on the Chart toolbar to toggle between displaying and hiding the data table.

NOTE

If you use a data table, you do not need a legend because the legend is built in. You can make the text in the data table bigger the same way that you did with the legend earlier.

Formatting Chart Elements

Each element of a chart has its own formatting settings. For example, the chart walls, chart floor, legend, each different colored bar or slice, each label, and each axis can be formatted separately. Just right-click on any element and choose its Format command from the shortcut menu. The exact name of the command depends on the chosen element.

The following sections show a few examples of this flexible procedure.

Changing Series Colors

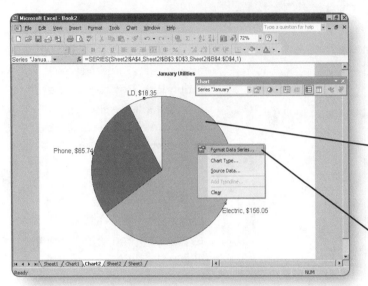

One series is distinguished from another by color. You can change the colors used in the chart to any colors you like (for example, your company's official colors).

1. Right-click on the **bar**, **slice**, or **other series shape** that you want to change. A shortcut menu will appear.

2. Click on **Format Data Series**. The Format Data Series dialog box will open.

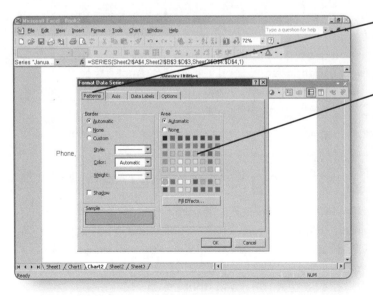

3. Click on the **Patterns tab**. The tab will come to the front if it is not already there.

4. Click on a **colored square** in the Area section to choose a new color. The new color will appear in the Sample area.

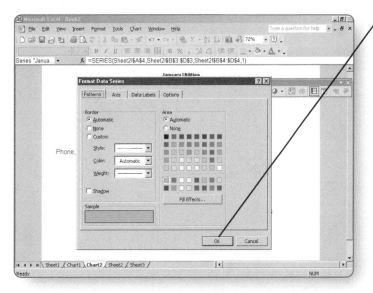

5. Click on **OK**. The new color will appear in the chart.

Setting a Number Format for an Axis

If the numbers on your value axis (usually the vertical axis) represent a certain unit, such as dollars, you may want to format them as such.

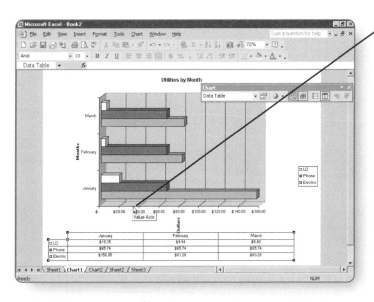

1. Point the **mouse** at the axis that contains the values. A ScreenTip will appear saying "Value Axis." If it says anything different, you are pointing at the wrong spot; reposition the pointer.

2. Right-click. A shortcut menu will appear.

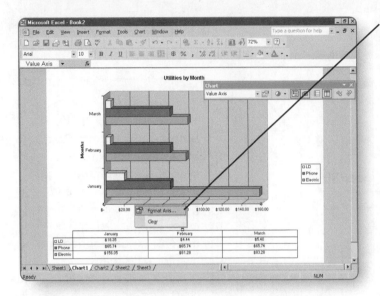

3. Click on **Format Axis**. The Format Axis dialog box will open.

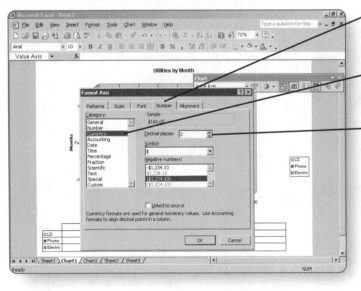

4. Click on the **Number tab**. The tab will come to the front.

5. Click on a **number format category**, such as Currency.

6. Click on the **up** and **down arrows** to change the number of Decimal places if desired.

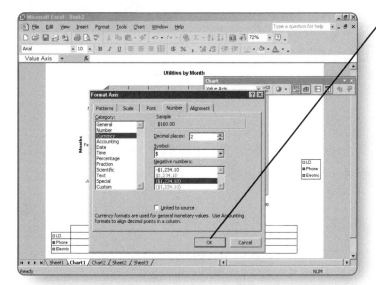

7. Click on **OK**. The dialog box will close, and the numbers on that axis will be formatted as you specified.

Part IV Review Questions

1. What is the difference between clip art and WordArt? *See "Adding WordArt" in Chapter 13*

2. What menu do you use to add clip art or WordArt to a worksheet? *See "Opening the Clip Art Controls" and "Adding WordArt" in Chapter 13*

3. How can you resize clip art after you've added it to a worksheet? *See "Adjusting the Size of Clip Art" in Chapter 13*

4. What toolbar contains buttons that enable you to change the look of a piece of clip art? *See "Adjusting the Quality of the Picture" in Chapter 13*

5. How do you access the Excel Chart Wizard? *See "Creating a Chart with the Chart Wizard" in Chapter 14*

6. How do you change a chart's type without re-creating it entirely? *See "Changing the Chart Type" in Chapter 14*

7. How do you switch between charting by rows and charting by columns? *See "Changing How the Data Is Plotted" in Chapter 14*

8. How do you make the chart refer to other cells? *See "Changing Which Cells Are Plotted" in Chapter 14*

9. How do you change the font used in the legend? *See "Resizing the Legend" in Chapter 15*

10. To format a part of the chart, you right-click it and then select what command? *See "Formatting Chart Elements" in Chapter 15*

PART V

Sharing with Other Programs and People

16

Integrating Excel with Word

Excel and Word work together smoothly so that you can easily combine an Excel worksheet with a Word document. For example, you can have a memo created in Word that contains an Excel worksheet. In this chapter, you'll learn how to:

- Create an Excel worksheet from within Word
- AutoFormat an Excel worksheet in Word
- Insert rows or columns in an Excel worksheet in Word
- Insert an existing Excel worksheet into a Word document
- Import Word data into Excel

Creating an Excel Worksheet from within Word

You can create a new Excel worksheet in a Word document using the Insert Microsoft Excel Worksheet button. The worksheet you create is actually part of the Word document, and when you save the Word file, this spreadsheet is saved as part of the document. This is called *embedding* a worksheet in Word.

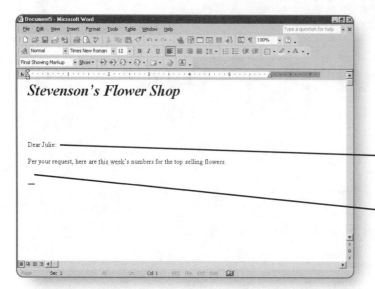

1. Type text in the Word document.

2. Click in the **Word document** where you want your Excel worksheet to appear. The insertion point will be placed.

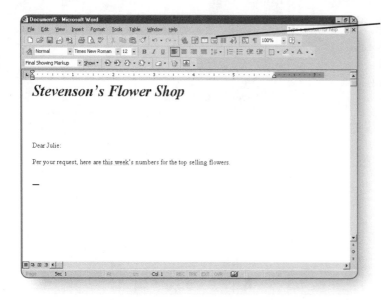

3. Click on the **Insert Microsoft Excel Worksheet button**. A grid of boxes will appear beneath the button.

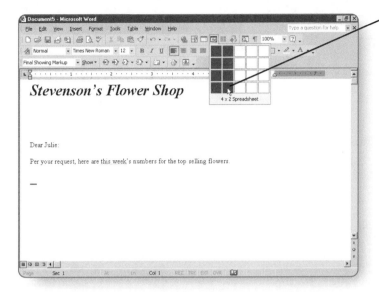

4. Move the **mouse pointer** over the grid until you see the number of columns and rows you want at the bottom of the grid.

5. Click to select the **number** of rows and columns.

An Excel screen containing a worksheet, menu bar, and toolbar will appear within the Word document, but the Microsoft Word title bar will remain.

6. Click in the **cell** where you want to enter data. The cell selector will appear around it.

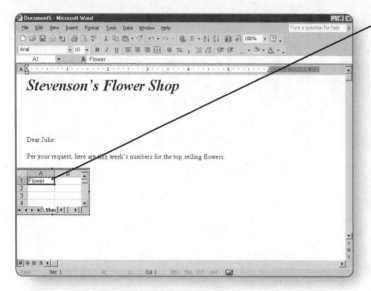

7. Enter the **data** you want to appear in that cell.

8. Press the **Enter key**. Excel will accept the data and move to the next cell.

TIP

If you accidentally click outside the Excel worksheet and the Excel tools disappear, double-click inside the worksheet area and they will reappear.

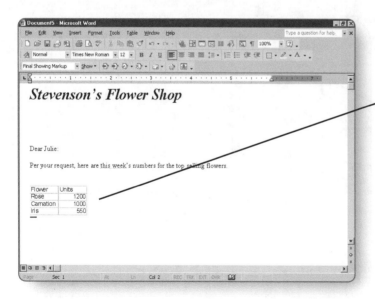

9. Repeat steps 6 through 8 until you have entered all the data you want in the worksheet.

10. Click on an **area outside the worksheet** to see how it will look in the Word document. The Excel tools will disappear and the Word tools will reappear.

AutoFormatting an Embedded Worksheet

When the embedded worksheet is active, the tools and buttons on the toolbar are Excel's, even though you're in Word. You can use them to format the worksheet the same way that you would use them in Excel. This includes AutoFormatting.

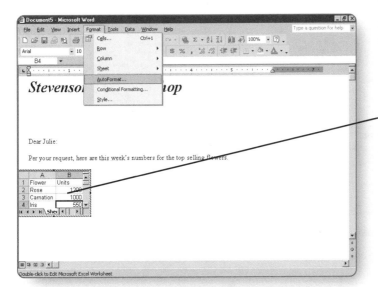

1. Double-click in the **Excel worksheet area**. The Excel tools will appear.

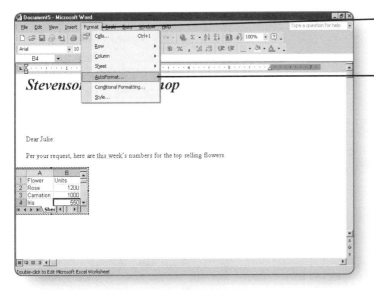

2. Click on **Format**. The Format menu will appear.

3. Click on **AutoFormat.** The AutoFormat dialog box will open.

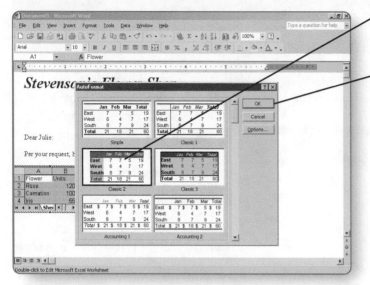

4. **Click** on a **format** that you want to use.

5. **Click** on **OK**. The AutoFormat dialog box will close.

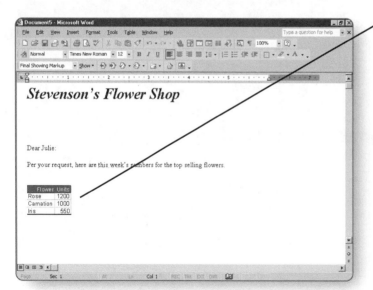

6. **Click** on an **area outside the worksheet**. The Excel tools will disappear and the Word tools will reappear.

NOTE

If only part of your worksheet appears, you may have accidentally scrolled it out of view. Double-click the worksheet to return to it, and then use the scroll bars in its window to bring your data into view. You can use the worksheet window's selection handles to enlarge its overall area in the document if desired.

Inserting Rows or Columns in an Embedded Worksheet

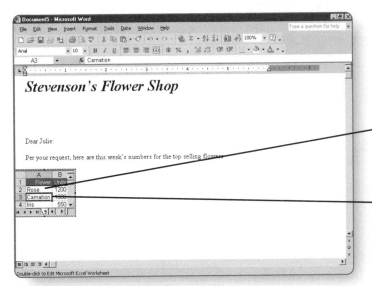

If you forget a row or column, you can use the Excel tools to insert the missing element, the same as you would in a regular worksheet.

1. **Double-click** the **embedded worksheet**. The Excel tools will appear.

2. **Click** in the **cell** where you want the new row or column to appear. The cell will be selected.

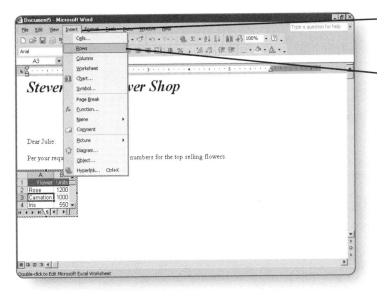

3. **Click** on **Insert**. The Insert menu will appear.

4. **Click** on **Rows** or **Columns** depending on what you want to insert.

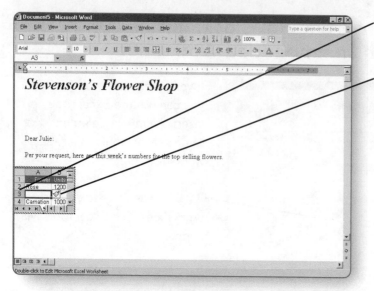

The new row or column will appear.

The Format Painter icon indicates the availability of a drop-down list for formatting.

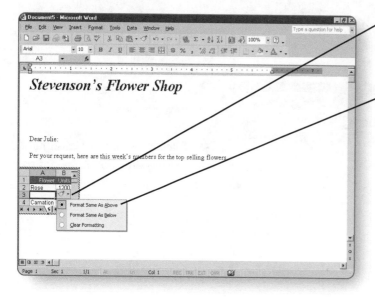

5. **Click** on the **Format Painter** button next to the inserted area. A menu will appear.

6. **Click** a **menu selection** to paint the inserted area to match surrounding cells.

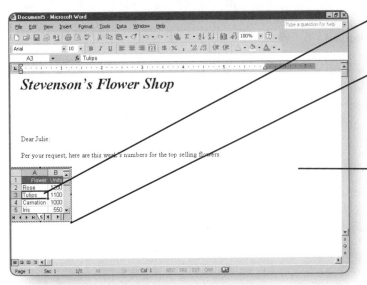

7. Type the **data** in the new row or column.

8. Drag the **selection handles** of the Excel worksheet. The worksheet will expand so all rows and columns are visible.

9. Click outside the **Excel worksheet**. The display will return to Word.

Inserting an Existing Excel Worksheet into Word

You also can insert entire existing Excel worksheets into Word documents, embedding the worksheets or linking them. Linking files means that changes you make in the worksheet in the Excel file will also appear in the Word file that contains the link.

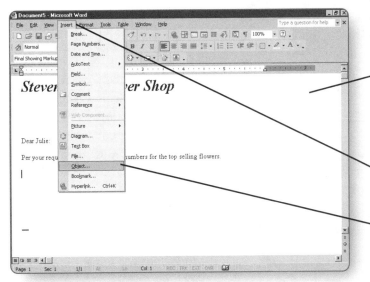

1. Click in the **Word document** where you want your Excel worksheet to appear. The insertion point will be placed.

2. Click on **Insert**. The Insert menu will appear.

3. Click on **Object**. The Object dialog box will open.

4. **Click** on the **Create from File** tab. The tab will come to the front.

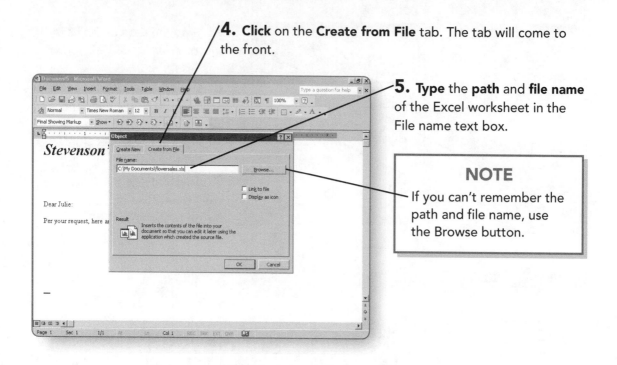

5. **Type** the **path** and **file name** of the Excel worksheet in the File name text box.

NOTE

If you can't remember the path and file name, use the Browse button.

6. **Click** on either or both of the following **check box options**:

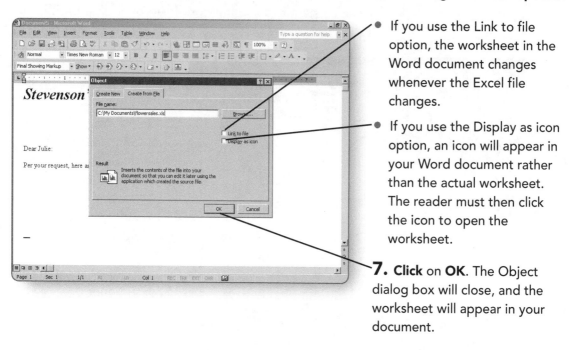

- If you use the Link to file option, the worksheet in the Word document changes whenever the Excel file changes.

- If you use the Display as icon option, an icon will appear in your Word document rather than the actual worksheet. The reader must then click the icon to open the worksheet.

7. **Click** on **OK**. The Object dialog box will close, and the worksheet will appear in your document.

Linking a Part of an Existing Excel Sheet

If you want to link only certain cells from an Excel sheet, you must use the Paste Special command.

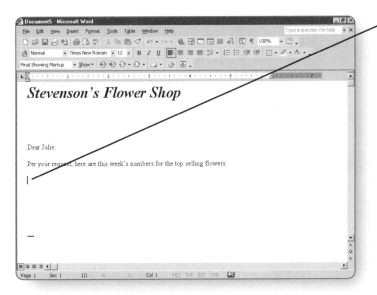

1. In Word, **position** the **insertion point** where you want the Excel cells to appear.

2. Click the **Minimize button**. The Word screen will be minimized.

3. In Excel, **open** the **workbook** from which you want to link cells.

4. Select the **cells** you want to use. The cells will be highlighted.

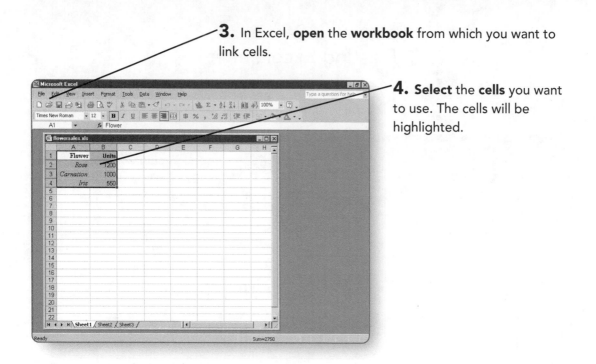

5. Click on **Edit**. The Edit menu will appear.

6. Click on **Copy**. The cells will be copied to the Clipboard.

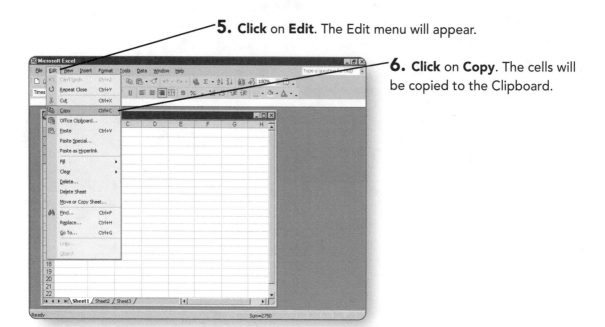

7. **Click** on the **Word document** in the taskbar. The Word window will reopen.

8. **Click** on **Edit**. The Edit menu will appear.

9. **Click** on **Paste Special**. The Paste Special dialog box will open.

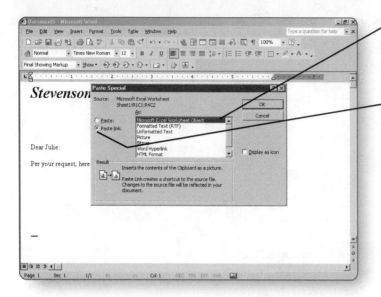

10. **Click** on **Microsoft Excel Worksheet Object** in the As list. The item will be selected.

11. **Click** on **Paste link**. The option button will be selected.

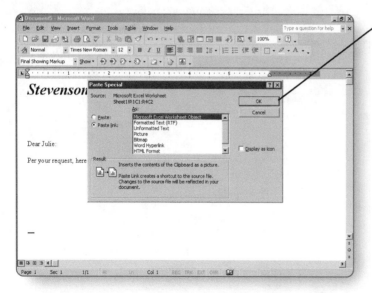

12. **Click** on **OK**. The cells will be pasted into your Word document.

NOTE

By choosing Paste link in step 11, you create a link between the original Excel file and the Word file, so that when the Excel copy changes, the Word copy will too. If you don't want that, choose Paste in step 11 instead, or simply choose the Paste command instead of Paste Special in step 9.

Importing Word Data into Excel

Data can go both ways between Excel and Word. You can also place Word data into Excel. After completing the earlier exercises in this chapter, you already have all the skills you need to do so.

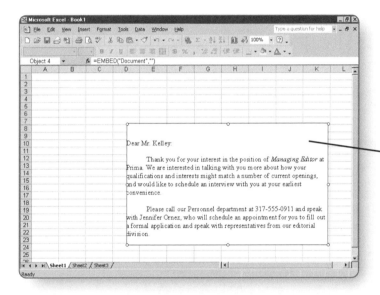

You can use the same technique described in "Inserting an Existing Excel Worksheet into Word" to insert a Word document into Excel with the Insert, Object command.

When you do so, the Word document is placed as a floating object above the cells, much like a chart. You double-click it to edit it.

If you want to be able to edit the Word document's text in Excel cells, you should use Copy and Paste to transfer the data. To create a link between the two files, use Paste Special instead of Paste, as you learned in "Linking a Part of an Existing Excel Sheet."

If you copy and paste regular paragraphs of a document into Excel, they are placed in a single column, with one paragraph per cell.

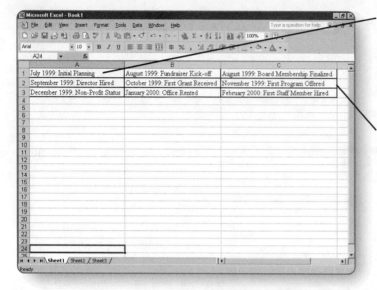

If you copy and paste a Word table, or tablelike text with the columns separated by tabs or commas, the data is placed in multiple columns.

Cell formatting came from the formatting of the table in Word.

17

Integrating Excel with Access

Excel and Access are a natural team because they both work with data in a row-and-column format. Access tables are very much like Excel worksheets, so you can easily transfer data between the two programs to take advantage of specific program features. For example, Excel is great for formula creation, so you might want to do most of your data calculation and analysis in Excel. Access has superior filtering and querying capabilities, so you might want to use Access for those tasks.

In this chapter, you'll learn how to:

- Import Excel data into Access
- Link an Excel worksheet to Access
- Export an Access table or query to Excel

Importing Excel Data into Access

You can import data from an Excel worksheet into an existing Access table, or you can create a new table in Access based on that worksheet.

NOTE

The following sections assume a basic knowledge of Access concepts such as databases, records, datasheets, and table design. If you need more help with Access, see the book *Access 2002 Fast & Easy*.

Beginning a Data Import from Excel to Access

Whether you want to place the incoming data in a new table or append it to an existing one, the procedure starts out the same.

1. Open the **Access database** in Access.

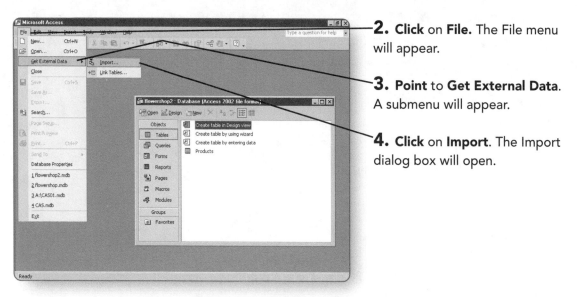

2. Click on **File**. The File menu will appear.

3. Point to **Get External Data**. A submenu will appear.

4. Click on **Import**. The Import dialog box will open.

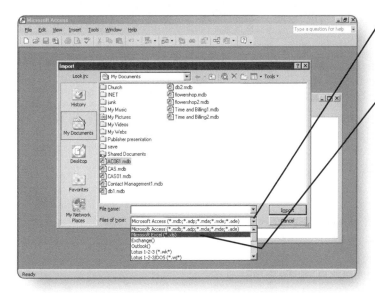

5. Click on the **down arrow** next to Files of type. A drop-down list will open.

6. Click on **Microsoft Excel (*.xls).** Microsoft Excel (*.xls) will appear in the Files of type box.

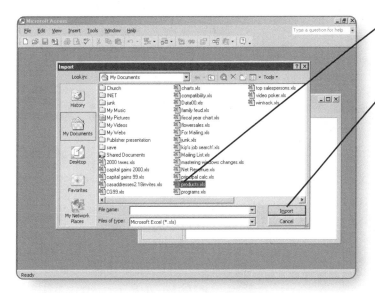

7. Click on the **Excel workbook** from which you want to import. It will be selected.

8. Click on **Import**. The Import Spreadsheet Wizard will open.

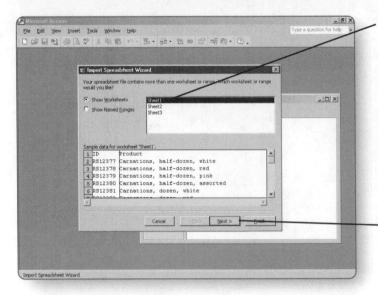

9. Click on the **worksheet name** containing the data to import. Its data will appear in the sample area.

NOTE

You can import from only one sheet at a time.

10. Click on **Next**. The next screen of the wizard will appear.

11. Click on **First Row Contains Column Headings** if the first row of the worksheet contains field names. The first row of the sample area will become shaded, indicating it does not contain data.

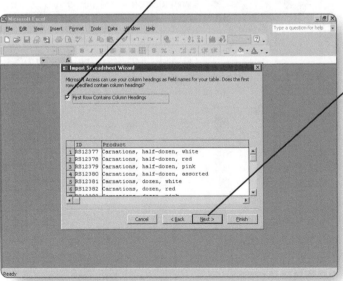

12. Click on **Next**.

13. Use one of the following procedures, depending on what you want to do next:

- To create a new table with the data, see "Importing Excel Data as a New Table."

- To append data to an existing table, see "Appending Excel Data to an Existing Table."

Importing Excel Data as a New Table

If the incoming data does not belong in any existing table in the database, you can create a new table. This is the simplest import method because it does not have any restrictions on existing fields matching up to imported ones or data being of a certain type. Access will automatically create a field for each column in the worksheet being imported and will set the data type appropriately for the data it finds there.

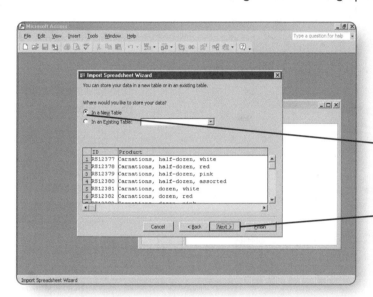

1. Click the **In a New Table** option button if it is not already selected.

2. Click on **Next**. The next screen of the Import Spreadsheet Wizard will ask you to specify information about each field being imported.

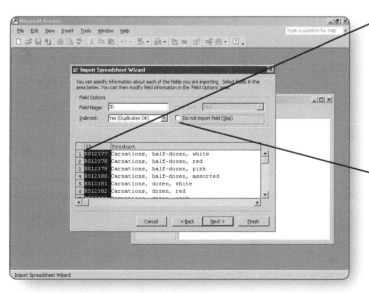

It starts with the leftmost column in the worksheet, which appears highlighted. You can set values for other columns by clicking the column you want in the sample area before performing the next steps.

If you do not want to import a particular field, mark the Do not import field (Skip) check box for that field and then skip to step 6.

3. **Type** or **edit** the **field name** in the Field Name box.

By default, this is the name of the column heading, if you specified that the first row contained column headings. If you did not, the field name will be blank and you must enter one.

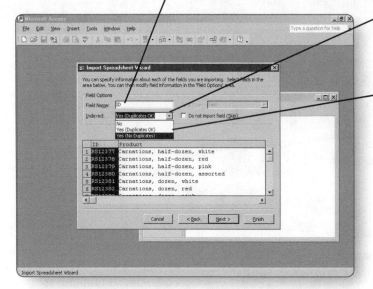

4. **Click** the **down arrow** next to Indexed. A drop-down list will appear.

5. **Click** on an **indexing option** for the field. Your choices are:

- **No**. Does not index the field.

- **Yes (Duplicates OK)**. Indexes the field and allows more than one record to have the same value for that field.

- **Yes (No Duplicates)**. Indexes the field and forces each record to have a unique value for the field.

NOTE

Indexing is a feature in Access that prepares the table for faster searching by creating an alphabetical index of the values in that field that Access can use when you search or sort by that field. The index is an internal object that you cannot access as a separate object in Access. Indexing is not important unless your table is rather large (over 1,000 records or so).

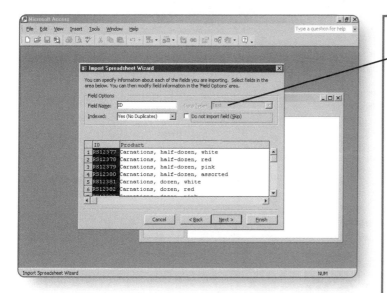

NOTE

If it's available, you can choose a data type from the Data Type drop-down list. This setting will not be available unless all the data in that column in Excel matches the requirements for a particular data type, such as all-numeric for the Numeric data type, or all 0 or 1 (or Yes/No or True/False) for the Logical data type, or all valid dates for the Date/Time data type.

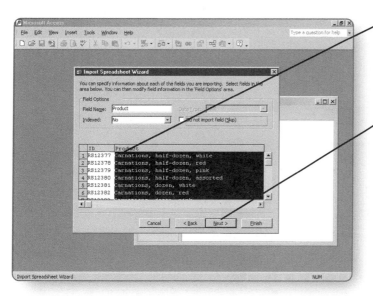

6a. **Click** on the **next column** you want to set up, and then return to step 3.

OR

6b. **Click** on **Next** when you have finished setting up all fields to be imported. You will be asked to specify a primary key field.

The *primary key* field is the unique field in the table that differentiates one record from another. It is not required but is strongly recommended.

7. Choose one of the following:

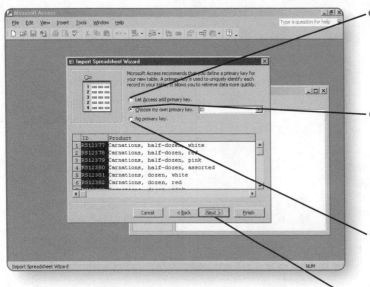

- **Let Access add primary key**. If none of the existing fields contain unique data for each record, but you want to use a primary key field.

- **Choose my own primary key**. If an existing field is appropriate for use as a primary key. Then choose the field you want from the drop-down list.

- **No primary key**. If this table does not need to have a primary key.

8. Click on **Next**. You will be prompted to enter a table name.

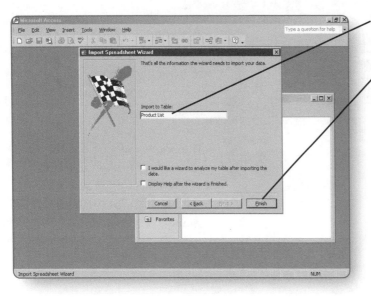

9. Type a **name** for the new table in the Import to Table box.

10. Click on **Finish**. A confirmation box will appear.

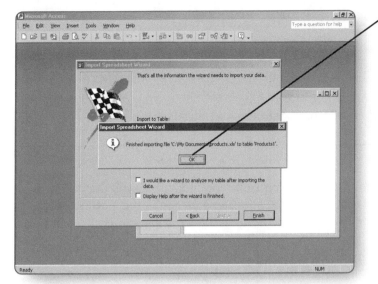

11. Click on **OK**. The table will be created.

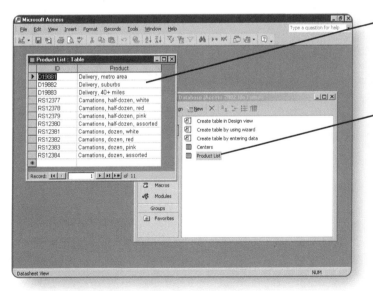

The new table will appear on the Tables list in the Database window. To view it, double-click the table name.

The new table will appear in Datasheet view in a window within Access.

Appending Excel Data to an Existing Table

If the fields in the existing Access table match up exactly with the columns in your Excel worksheet, you can append rows from the Excel sheet as new records in the table.

CAUTION

In order to successfully append from Excel, the columns must have exactly the same names as the existing fields in the table, and none of the incoming data can violate any restrictions or limitations set up in Access. For example, text cannot be placed in a field with a Numeric field type, and duplicate values cannot be entered in a primary key field. The operation will fail if there is a type mismatch or rule violation.

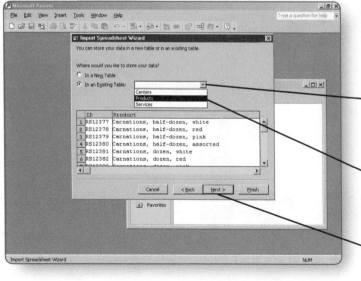

The following steps pick up from the section "Beginning a Data Import from Excel to Access" earlier in the chapter.

1. **Click** the **down arrow** next to In an Existing Table. A drop-down list will appear.

2. **Click** the **existing table** into which you want to import. Its name will appear in the box.

3. **Click** on **Next**.

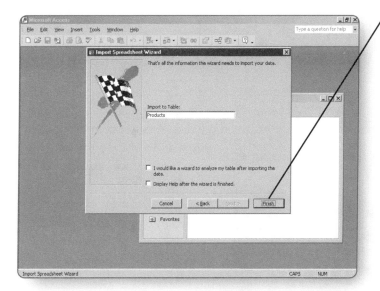

4. **Click** on **Finish**. A confirmation box will appear.

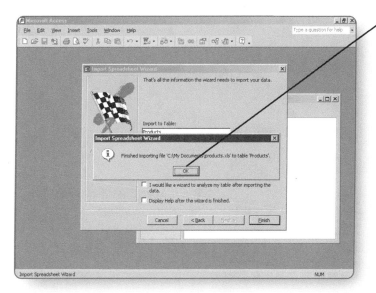

5. **Click** on **OK**. The table will be created.

Linking an Excel Worksheet to Access

If you would like to keep using the Excel worksheet, but also use its data in Access, you can create a link between the Excel worksheet and the Access database. This can come in handy if you plan to update the data in Excel periodically as well as use it in Access, because you won't have to reimport it every time you want a fresh copy in Access.

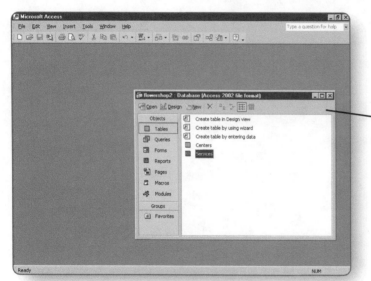

1. Open the **Access database** in Access.

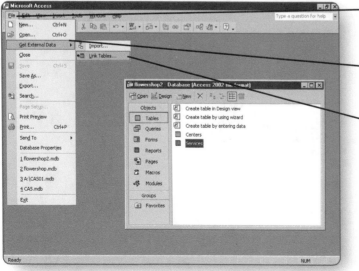

2. Click on **File.** The File menu will appear.

3. Point to **Get External Data.** A submenu will appear.

4. Click on **Link Tables**. The Link dialog box will open.

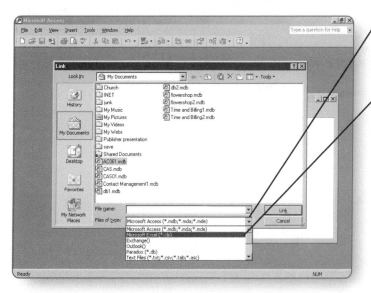

5. Click on the **down arrow** next to Files of type. A dropdown list will open.

6. Click on **Microsoft Excel (*.xls)**. Microsoft Excel (*.xls) will appear in the Files of type box.

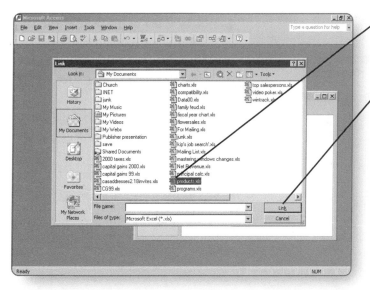

7. Click on the **Excel workbook** that you want to link. It will be selected.

8. Click on **Link**. The Link Spreadsheet Wizard will open.

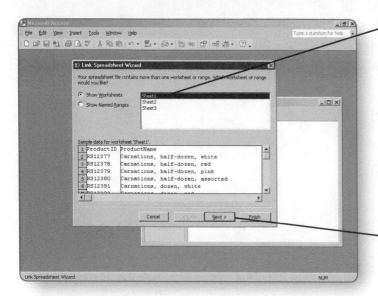

9. Click on the **worksheet name** containing the data to link. Its data will appear in the sample area.

> **NOTE**
>
> You can link only one sheet at a time.

10. Click on **Next**. The next screen of the wizard will appear.

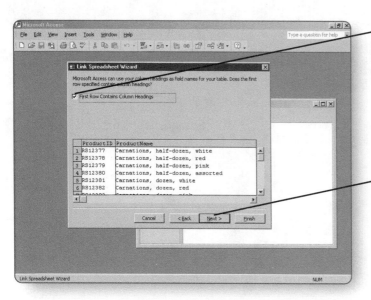

11. Click on **First Row Contains Column Headings** if the first row of the worksheet contains field names. The first row of the sample area will become shaded, indicating it does not contain data.

12. Click on **Next**.

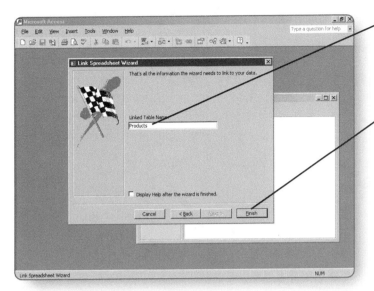

13. **Type** a **name** for the link. It need not be the same as the workbook file name or sheet name.

14. **Click** on **Finish**. A confirmation box will appear.

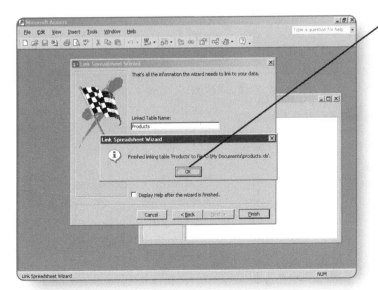

15. **Click** on **OK**. The worksheet will be linked.

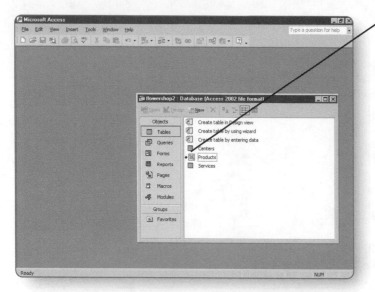

The linked worksheet will appear on the Tables list in the Database window, and you can work with it just like any other table in Access. It has a different icon from the other tables, to help you remember that it is a link.

Exporting an Access Table or Query to Excel

When you want to use Excel to work with Access data, you can easily export an Access table or query to Excel. There are several ways to do this, but one of the easiest is to use the Office Links feature.

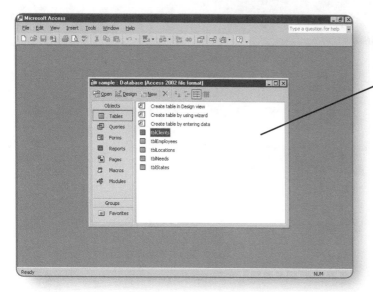

1. Open the **database** in Access that contains the table or query you want to export to Excel.

2. **Click Tables** or **Queries**, depending on which you want to export.

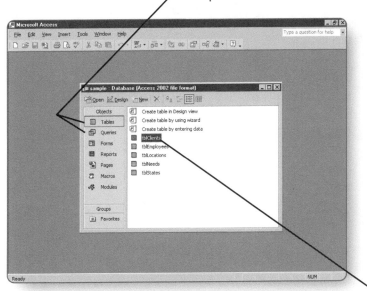

NOTE

A *query*, in simple terms, is a saved sort/filter operation that takes records from a table and displays them according to criteria you specify. The results of a query look just like a table, but contain fewer records or fields than the original or are sorted in a specific way.

3. **Double-click** the **table** or **query**. The table or query will open in Datasheet view.

4. **Click** on **Tools**. The Tools menu will appear.

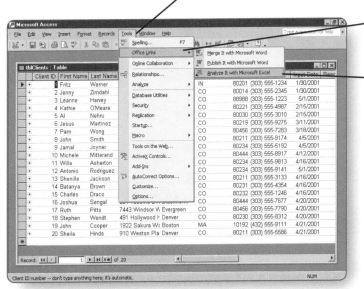

5. **Point** to **Office Links**. A submenu will appear.

6. **Click** on **Analyze It with Microsoft Excel**. Excel will open and the chosen table from Access will display as a sheet in a new workbook in Excel.

The Excel file is already saved with the Access table's name, in the same location as the Access database from which it came.

18

Using Excel to Analyze Data from the Web

As you browse the Internet, you might find data that would be useful to analyze using Excel's advanced sorting and calculation capabilities. There are several ways to get that data into Excel, either as a one-time Paste operation or as a refreshable link that you can update whenever you are connected. You'll learn about them in this chapter, which teaches you how to:

- Open a Web document in Excel
- Copy data from a Web page
- Run a Web query

Opening Web Documents in Excel

If you already have a Web (HTML) document on your hard disk, you can open it in Excel and edit or analyze it there.

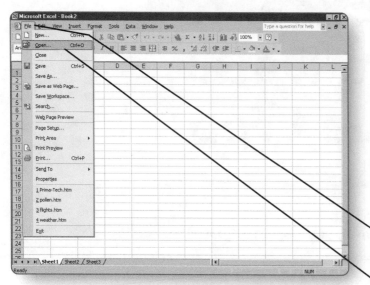

NOTE

This procedure opens an entire Web page in Excel. If you want only a specific portion of a Web page to appear in Excel, try Copy and Paste instead, as described in the following section.

1. Click on **File**. The File menu will appear.

2. Click on **Open.** The Open dialog box will open.

3. Navigate to the **drive or folder** containing the file to open.

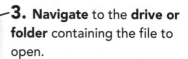

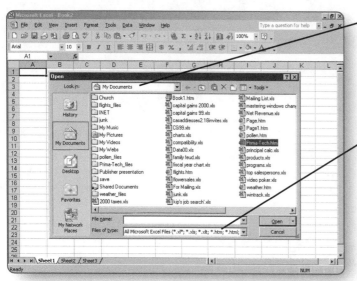

NOTE

You don't have to change the file type because by default Excel includes .htm and .html files in its file listing.

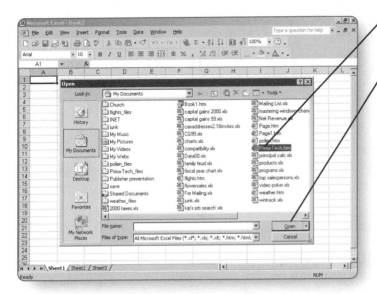

4. Click on the **file** you want to open. It will be selected.

5. Click on **Open**. The file will open in Excel.

Depending on the file, the format might not appear exactly as it does in a Web browser. That's because when the data imports into Excel, it is forced into rows and columns, and not all data looks good that way.

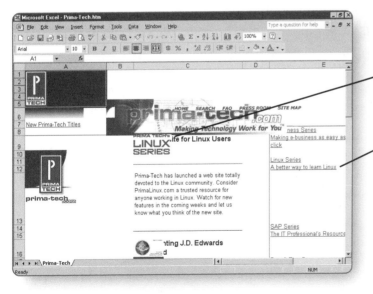

Some data might appear truncated because of cell width limitations.

Any hyperlinks remain hyperlinks, so you can click on them within Excel to open the linked content in your Web browser.

Copying Data from a Web Page

You don't have to save entire Web pages for use in Excel; you can pick individual elements from Web pages and include them in Excel. For example, when you visit a weather forecasting site, you might just want the weather for your area, and not all the advertisements, hyperlinks, and headings surrounding it.

NOTE

It is your responsibility to make sure you do not violate any copyrights when exporting or copying data from Web sites.

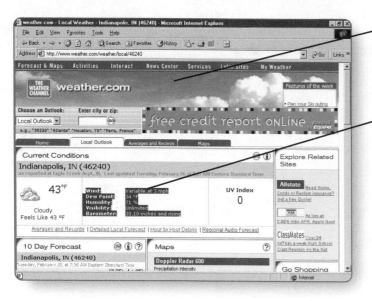

1. Display the **page** from which you want to copy in your Web browser program (such as Internet Explorer).

2a. Drag the **mouse** across the text to select. It will appear selected.

OR

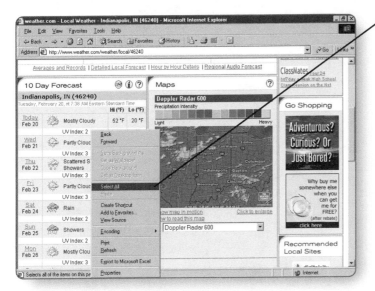

2b. Right-click an **area** and **choose Select All** to select an entire frame, table, or other section.

NOTE

Ctrl+A is a shortcut for the Select All command, but right-clicking and choosing Select All is better on pages containing multiple frames because you can right-click the frame you want.

3. Click on **Edit**. The Edit menu will appear.

4. Click on **Copy**. The selection will be copied to the Clipboard.

5. Minimize the **Web browser window**.

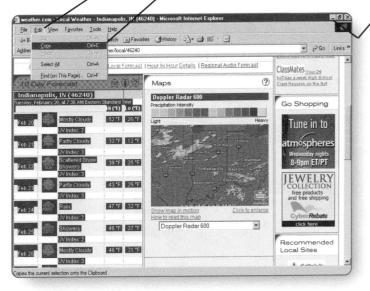

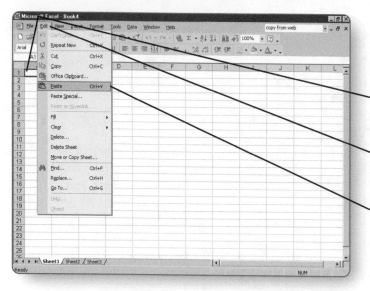

6. Open the **workbook** in Excel where you want to paste, or **start** a **new workbook**.

7. Click on the **cell** into which you want to paste.

8. Click on **Edit**. The Edit menu will appear.

9. Click on **Paste**. The selection will be pasted into the workbook at the location you chose.

10. Click on the **Clipboard icon** in the bottom right corner of the pasted selection. A menu will appear.

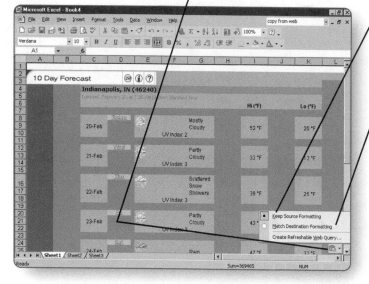

11a. Click on **Keep Source Formatting** to copy the formatting of the Web page.

OR

11b. Click on **Match Destination Formatting** to apply the formatting from the Excel cells.

NOTE

You can also choose Create Refreshable Web Query in step 11 to make the data into a simple Web query, like the ones you will learn about in the following section.

Creating a Simple Web Query

A *Web query* is a link to external data on the Web. Unlike the simple Copy and Paste that you just learned about, a Web query actually contains links to the data source, so that you can update it in Excel with the latest data from the Web. Web queries do not include formatting, pictures, or the contents of scripts.

You can create a simple Web query by exporting data from the Web to Excel using the Export feature. This method exports a single table from a single Web page. The data must be in table format on the Web page for this to work.

1. Display the **page** from which you want to copy in Internet Explorer.

2. Right-click the **table** on the Web page that you want to copy to Excel. A shortcut menu will appear.

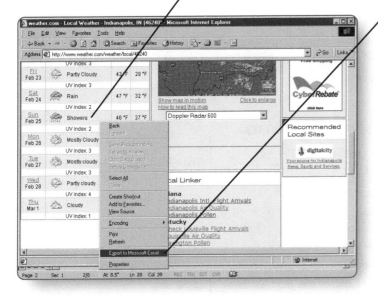

3. Click on **Export to Microsoft Excel**. The data will appear in a new Excel workbook.

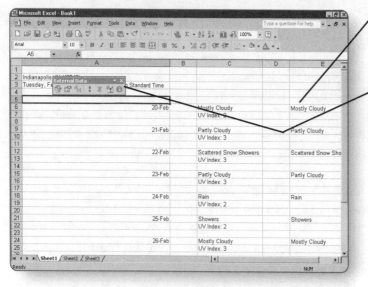

The formatting does not transfer—only the data transfers.

The External Data toolbar will also appear. See "Refreshing a Web Query" later in this chapter to learn how to use it.

Creating a Multi-Table Web Query

To create a more sophisticated Web query that can include multiple tables from a Web page, you can start either from a Web page or from Excel. The methods converge after the first few steps.

Starting a Web Query from a Web Page

If you already have the Web page on-screen that you want to use, you can start your Web query from there using the Edit With feature.

NOTE

The Edit With feature is not available on all Web pages. If the Edit With button is unavailable on the toolbar, try creating the Web query starting from within Excel, as described in the next section.

1. Display the **Web page** from which you want to query data in Internet Explorer.

2. Click the **arrow** next to the Edit With button on the toolbar. A menu will appear.

3. Click on **Edit with Microsoft Excel**. The Create New Web Query dialog box will open.

4. See "Finishing a Web Query."

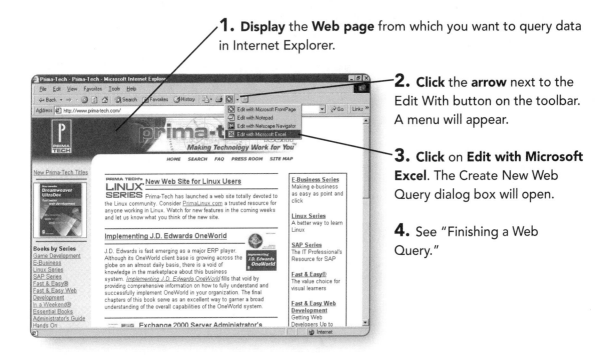

Starting a Web Query from Excel

You can also create a new Web query from within Excel itself.

1. Click on **Data**. The Data menu will appear.

2. Point to **Import External Data**. A submenu will appear.

3. Click on **New Web Query**. The New Web Query dialog box will open.

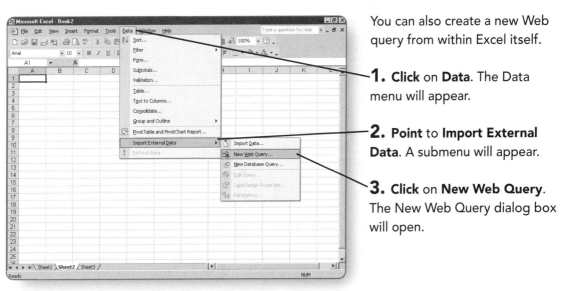

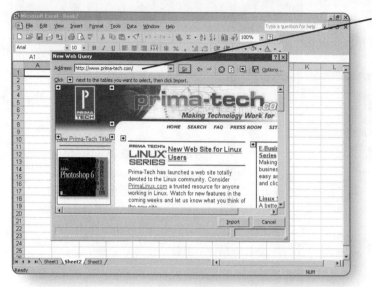

4. Type the **URL** for the Web page from which you want to get data. The page's content will appear in the window.

5. See "Finishing a Web Query."

Finishing a Web Query

This procedure starts when the New Web Query dialog box opens on-screen. The New Web Query dialog box shows each section of the Web page as a separate table. You choose which table(s) you want to import and then import them.

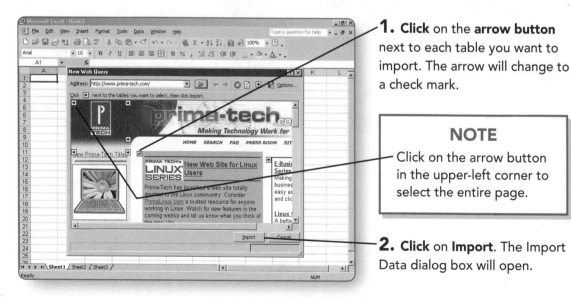

1. Click on the **arrow button** next to each table you want to import. The arrow will change to a check mark.

NOTE

Click on the arrow button in the upper-left corner to select the entire page.

2. Click on **Import**. The Import Data dialog box will open.

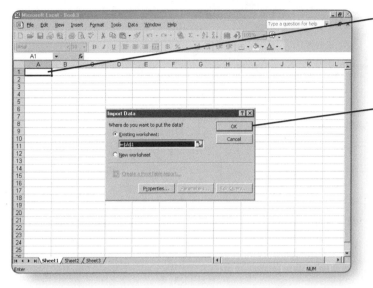

3. Click on the **cell** that should form the upper-right corner of the pasted area. Its address will appear in the box.

4. Click on **OK**. The data will appear in Excel. Formatting is not copied.

Refreshing a Web Query

The whole point of a Web query is to be able to refresh it with the latest data from the Web.

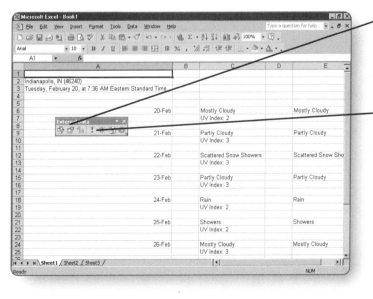

1. Display the **worksheet** containing the Web query's current data. The External Data toolbar will appear.

2. Click on the **Refresh Data button** on the External Data toolbar. The data will be refreshed.

Saving a Web Query

Web queries are automatically saved along with your workbook. You can also save a query so it can be run in other workbooks. Saved Web queries have an .iqy extension.

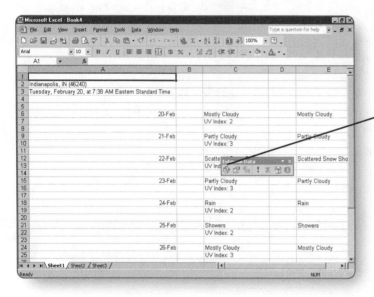

1. Display the **worksheet** containing the Web query's current data. The External Data toolbar will appear.

2. Click on the **Edit Query button** on the External Data toolbar. The Edit Web Query dialog box will open.

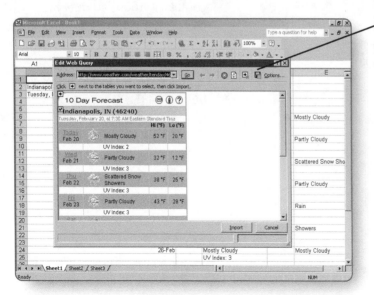

3. Click on the **Save Query button**. The Save As dialog box will open.

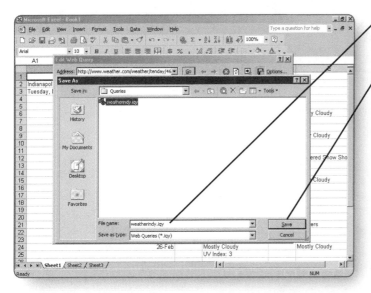

4. Type a **name** for the query in the File name box.

5. **Click** the **Save button**. The Edit Web Query dialog box will reopen.

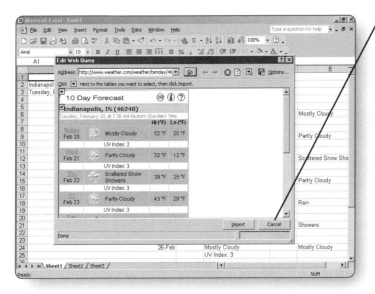

6. **Click** on **Cancel**. The dialog box will close.

Running a Saved Web Query

You can run any Web query you have saved, and also any of the various Web query samples that come with Excel.

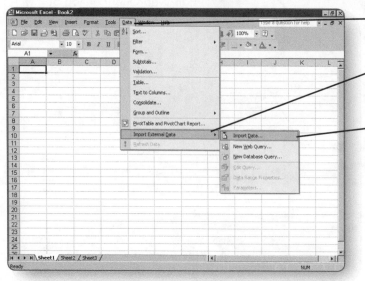

1. Click on **Data**. The Data menu will appear.

2. Point to **Import External Data**. A submenu will appear.

3. Click on **Import Data**. The Select Data Source dialog box will open. The My Data Sources folder is the default location shown.

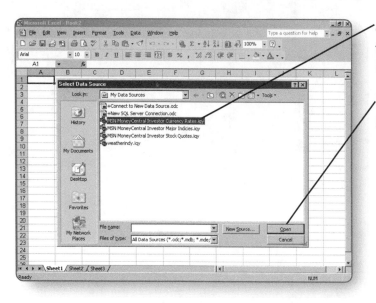

4. Click on the **query** you want to run. The ones that came with Excel start with MSN.

5. Click on **Open**. The Import Data dialog box will open.

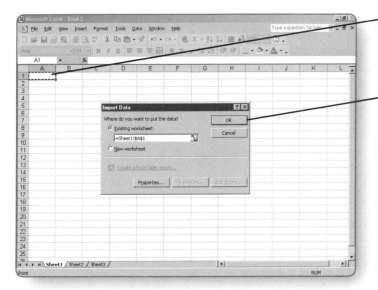

6. Click on the **cell** where you want the upper-left corner of the imported data to be.

7. Click on **OK**. The query results will appear in Excel.

NOTE

If you are not connected to the Internet when you run a Web query, you will be prompted to connect.

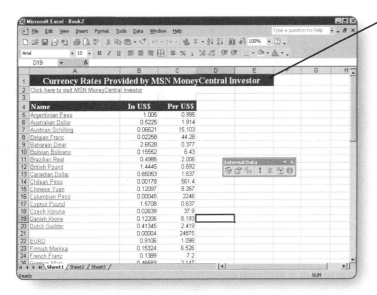

Notice that the results of the Microsoft-provided queries are nicely formatted, unlike the raw data you included in the Web queries you created. You can format the data in your Web queries using regular Excel formatting commands, and when you save the workbook, that formatting will be saved too.

19

Sharing Excel Data on the Internet

Like other Office applications, Excel has strong Web publishing capabilities that enable you to share your data with others in a format that anyone with a Web browser can use. That way, your audience need not have Excel in order to view your data. Excel also enables you to send data or even entire workbooks via e-mail. In this chapter, you'll learn how to:

- Insert a hyperlink
- Create an e-mail link
- Publish an Excel worksheet on the Web
- Send an Excel workbook via e-mail

Inserting a Hyperlink

As you may already know from exploring the Internet, many Web pages contain underlined strings of text that you can click on to jump to a specific Web page. These are called *hyperlinks*. A hyperlink can be text, or it can be attached to any other object, such as a picture or graph.

If you plan to publish your data in Web format, you might want to include hyperlinks in the worksheet that can provide access points to other resources on the Web. Even if you are not planning to save your Excel workbook in Web format, you might still want to include hyperlinks in it. For example, a hyperlink can provide a cross-reference to more information on a particular topic.

1. **Click** on the **cell** where you want to insert the hyperlink, or **select** the **graphic** or **chart**.

2. **Click** on **Insert**. The Insert menu will appear.

3. **Click** on **Hyperlink**. The Insert Hyperlink dialog box will open.

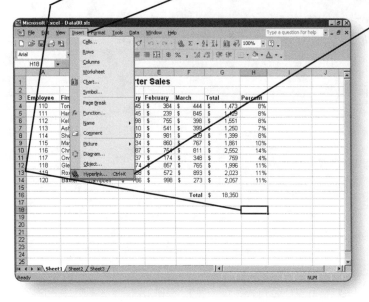

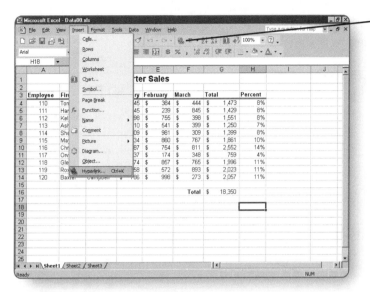

You can also click the Insert Hyperlink button instead of following steps 2 through 3.

4. Click on **Existing File or Web Page** in the Link to list.

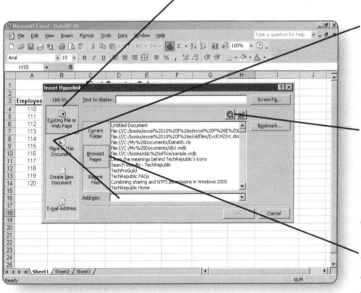

5a. **Type** the **address** of the Web page in the Address box, and **skip to step 8**.

OR

5b. **Click** on the **Web Page button** to browse for the Web page. Your Web browser program will open.

OR

5c. **Click** on **Browsed Pages**, and then **click** a **page name** and **skip to step 8**.

6. Navigate in your **Web browser** to the page to which you want to link.

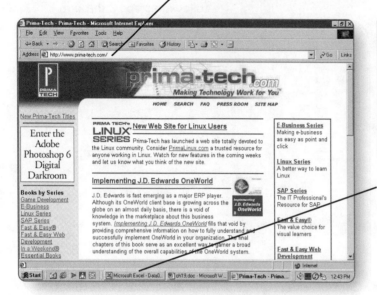

NOTE

You can use your Favorites list to choose a favorite page, or follow hyperlinks from your Start page to get to the page you want.

7. Click on **Microsoft Excel** on the Taskbar to switch back to Excel. The page's address will be filled in for you.

8. Type the **text** that you want to display in the Text to display box if the desired text does not already appear there.

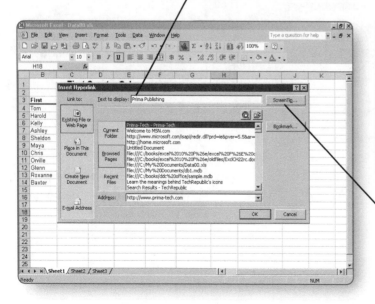

NOTE

The text you type in step 8 will be the underlined text that appears in the cell. If you type nothing here, the actual address will be used for the text.

9. (Optional) **Click** on the **ScreenTip button**. The Set Hyperlink ScreenTip dialog box will open.

10. Type text to use as a custom ScreenTip.

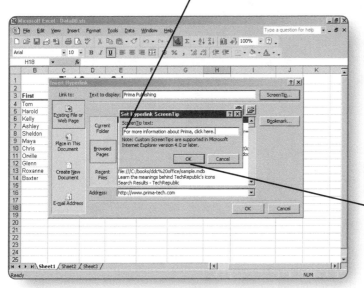

11. Click on **OK**. The Set Hyperlink ScreenTip dialog box will close.

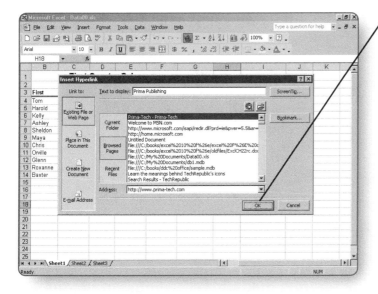

12. Click on **OK**. The hyperlink will appear in the cell.

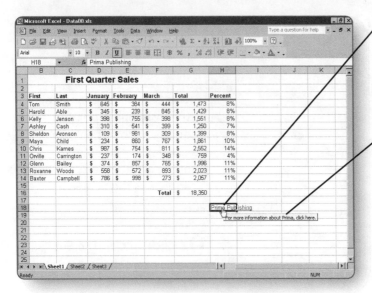

13. **Point** your **mouse** at the cell or object. A ScreenTip will appear showing the URL or whatever you entered for the ScreenTip in step 10.

14. **Click** on the **hyperlink**. Your Web browser will open and display the page.

15. **Click** on the **Close button** to close the Web browser.

Inserting an E-Mail Link

You can include a hyperlink that, instead of jumping to a Web page, opens a window in which an e-mail message can be composed and sent. This is handy if you want readers of your worksheet to be able to e-mail questions and comments to a certain person.

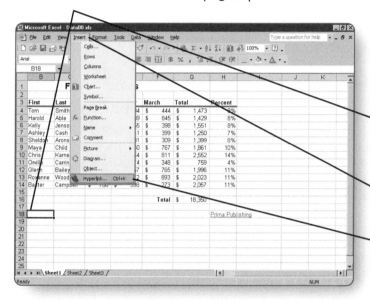

1. Click on the **cell** where you want the hyperlink to appear. The cell will be highlighted.

2. Click on **Insert**. The Insert menu will appear.

3. Click on **Hyperlink**. The Insert Hyperlink dialog box will open.

4. Click on **E-mail Address** in the Link to list.

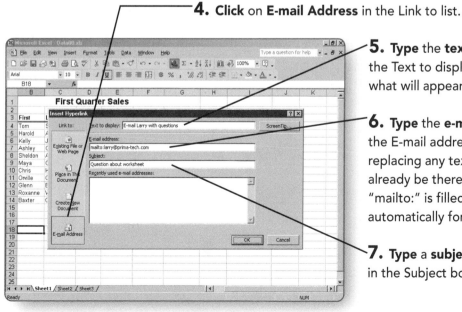

5. Type the **text** to display in the Text to display box. This is what will appear in the cell.

6. Type the **e-mail address** in the E-mail address box, replacing any text that may already be there. The word "mailto:" is filled in automatically for you.

7. Type a **subject** for the e-mail in the Subject box.

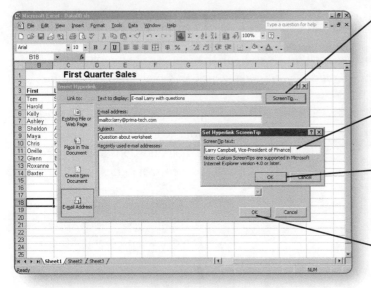

8. (Optional) **Click** on the **ScreenTip button**. The Set Hyperlink ScreenTip dialog box will open.

9. Type text to use as a custom ScreenTip.

10. Click on **OK**. The Set Hyperlink ScreenTip dialog box will close.

11. Click on **OK**. The link will be created.

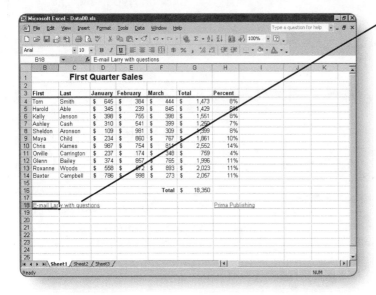

12. Click on the **hyperlink**. Your default e-mail program will open, displaying a new e-mail window.

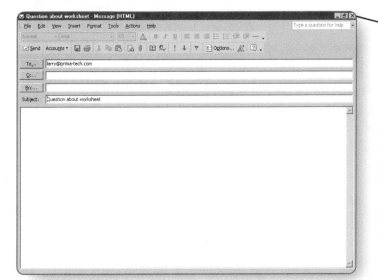

13. **Click** on the **Close button**. The e-mail program will close. (You don't actually want to send a message; you are just testing the link.)

NOTE

Depending on the e-mail program, you might be prompted to confirm that you want to close the message without sending or saving it.

Saving the Worksheet for the Web

When you save your worksheet in Web format, you make it possible for others who do not have Excel to view your data. All they need is a Web browser program.

You can save either in normal or interactive format. *Interactive* format allows visitors to the Web page to manipulate the data using a limited set of Excel tools. However, it requires that the visitor be using a recent version of Internet Explorer or Netscape Navigator in order to work. It also causes you to lose all noncell objects on the sheet, such as pictures or charts that float above the cells.

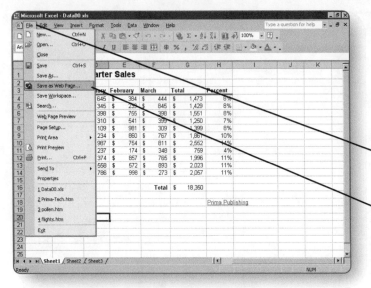

1. (Optional) **Select** the **range** of cells to save in Web format.

Do step 1 only if you do not want the entire active sheet or the entire workbook.

2. Click on **File**. The File menu will appear.

3. Click on **Save as Web Page**. The Save As dialog box will open.

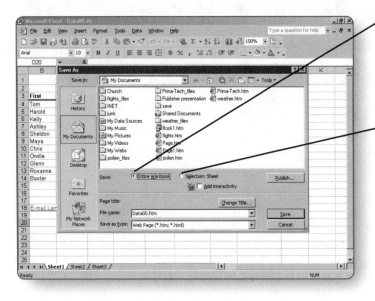

4a. Click on **Entire Workbook** to save the entire workbook (all sheets).

OR

4b. Click on **Selection** to save the selection.

If you did not select cells in step 1, the Selection is the sheet.

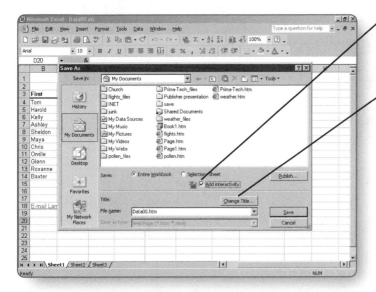

5. (Optional) **Click** on **Add interactivity**. A check mark will appear in the box.

6. Click on **Change Title**. The Set Title dialog box will open.

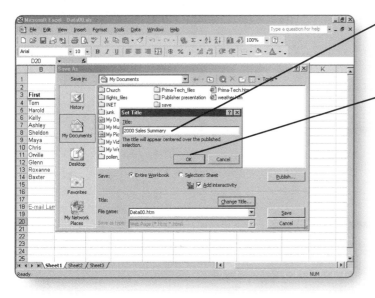

7. Type the **title** that you want to appear in the title bar when the Web page is displayed.

8. Click on **OK**. The Set Title dialog box will close.

9. Type a **file name** in the File name box. This name will be part of the page's Web address.

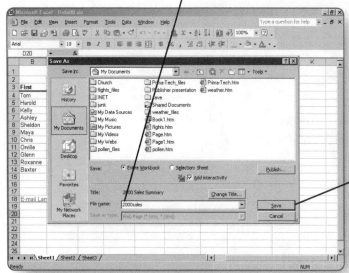

NOTE

You do not have to type .htm or .html at the end of the name in step 9; Excel will add that for you automatically.

10a. Click on **Save**. The page will be saved.

OR

10b. Jump to the **steps** in the next section, "Setting More Publishing Options," to view and change the publishing options.

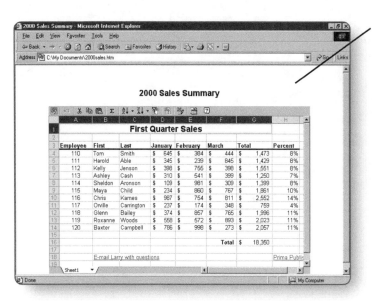

When your reader displays the page in a Web browser, if you chose to include user interactivity in step 5, the controls appear as shown here. Pointing the mouse pointer at each tool provides a ScreenTip that explains the tool's purpose.

NOTE

To publish the page on the Internet, you must copy it to an Internet *server*, a computer that is connected to the Internet. Ask your Internet service provider or your network administrator how to do this.

Setting More Publishing Options

Instead of clicking Save in step 10 of the previous section, you can do the following:

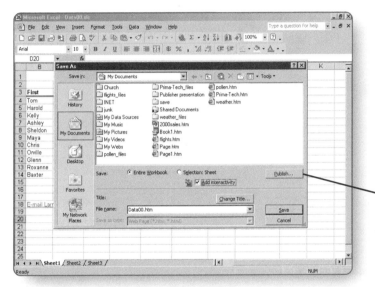

1. Click on **Publish**. The Publish as Web Page dialog box will open.

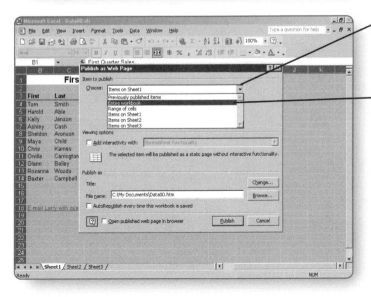

2. Click on the **down arrow** next to Choose. A list of options will appear.

3. Click on a **different item to publish** if desired.

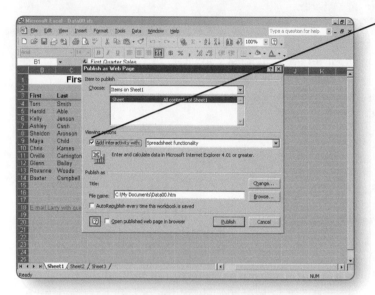

4a. **Click** on the **Add interactivity with check box** if you want interactivity. A check mark will appear in the box.

OR

4b. If you don't want interactivity, make sure that it is not marked, and then **skip to step 7**.

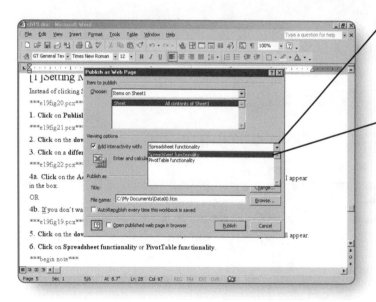

5. **Click** on the **down arrow** next to the Add interactivity with check box. A list of options will appear.

6. **Click** on **Spreadsheet functionality** or **PivotTable functionality**.

NOTE

PivotTable functionality gives the reader the ability to analyze the published data using Excel's PivotTable feature. For more information about PivotTables, see the Excel Help system.

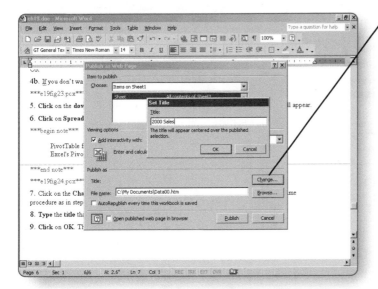

7. Click on the **Change button** to change the title if it is not correct or if it is blank. Use the same procedure as in steps 6–8 of the preceding procedure.

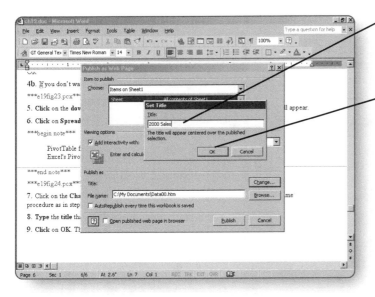

8. Type the **title** that you want to appear in the title bar when the Web page is displayed.

9. Click on **OK**. The Set Title dialog box will close.

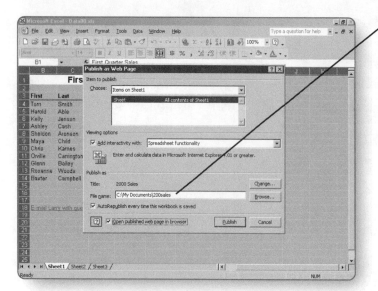

10. **Confirm** that the **file name** is correct. If it is not, type a different name in the File name box.

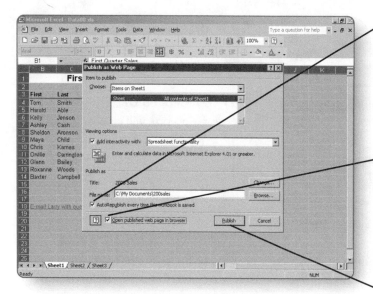

11. **Click** on the **AutoRepublish every time this workbook is saved check box** if you want to automatically update the HTML version whenever the original Excel file changes.

12. **Click** on the **Open published web page in browser check box** if you want to view the published file in your Web browser immediately after publishing.

13. **Click** on **Publish**. If you chose the check box in step 12, the page will open in your Web browser, for your inspection.

Sharing Excel Data via E-Mail

If you need to distribute data from an Excel workbook via e-mail, you can use the built-in tools in Excel to do so quickly and easily. You can either send the data in the body of an e-mail or attach the entire workbook as an e-mail attachment.

NOTE

Excel interacts with your default e-mail program. This might be Outlook, as shown in the figures in this chapter, or it might be some other program, such as Microsoft Exchange, Outlook Express, or cc:Mail.

Including Excel Data in an E-Mail Message Body

If you want to send only a part of your workbook via e-mail, you can include it in the body of an e-mail message.

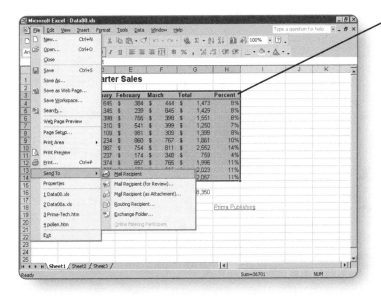

1. Select the **data** that you want to send.

2. Click on **File**. The File menu will appear.

3. Point to **Send To**. A submenu will appear.

4. Click on **Mail Recipient**. A mail composition screen will appear within Excel.

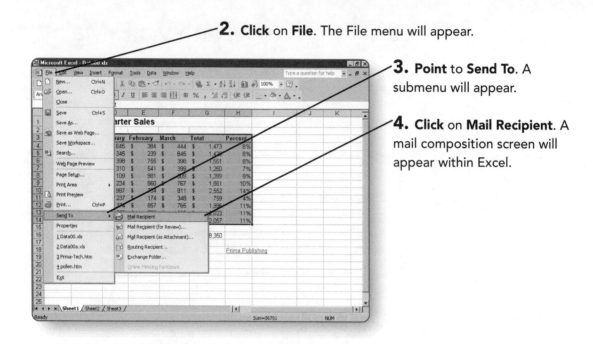

5. Type the **e-mail address** of the recipient.

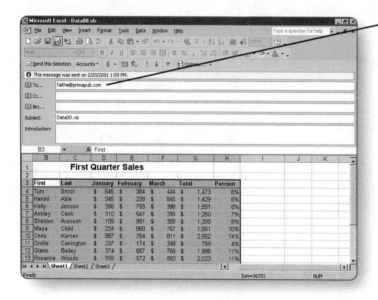

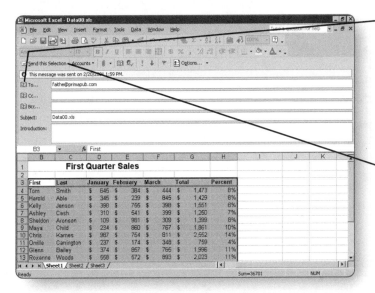

Depending on your e-mail program, you might also be able to look up the address in your address book. For example, with Outlook you can click the To button to open an address book.

6. Click on **Send this Selection**. The message will be sent.

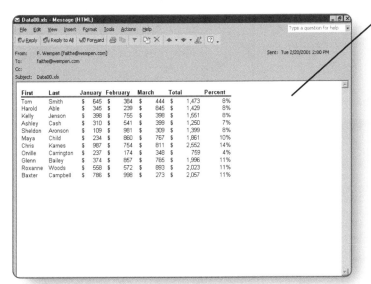

When the message is received, the gridlines from Excel do not appear.

CAUTION

The message you create this way might not be readable in all e-mail programs. If your recipient has difficulty with the received message, try sending the data as an attachment instead, as in the following section.

Attaching an Excel Workbook to an E-Mail Message

Since not all e-mail programs can read the embedded Excel data you learned about in the preceding section, you should also know how to send Excel files as e-mail attachments.

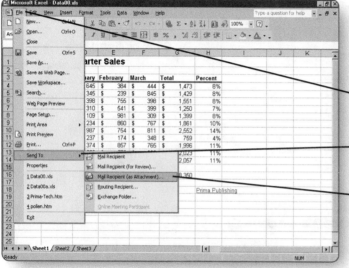

1. **Open** the **workbook** that you want to send.

2. **Click** on **File**. The File menu will appear.

3. **Point** to **Send To**. A submenu will appear.

4. **Click** on **Mail Recipient (as Attachment)**. Your default e-mail program will open, start a new message, and attach the file to it.

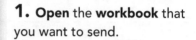

The attached file appears here in Outlook 2002; your e-mail program may look different.

5. **Type** the **e-mail address** of the recipient, or **look it up** in your e-mail program's address book.

6. (Optional) **Type** a **message** in the message composition area.

7. **Click** on **Send**. The message will be sent via your e-mail program.

20

Collaborating with Others

Excel 2002 offers several features aimed at making it easier for people to work as a group on a spreadsheet. You can add comments to individual cells, track the revisions that a workbook goes through as multiple people edit it, and protect certain cells from having changes made to them. In this chapter, you'll learn how to:

- Add comments to a cell
- Track revisions to a workbook
- Set worksheet/workbook protection

Working with Comments

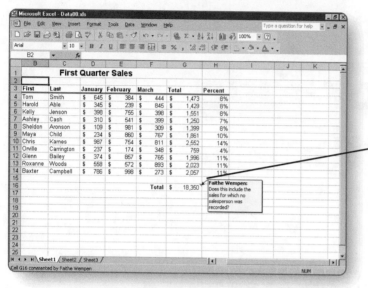

Comments enable people reviewing a worksheet to enter their thoughts and questions as attachments to individual cells without changing the formatting or appearance of the sheet.

When a cell has an attached comment, a triangle appears in its corner. You can point at the triangle to see the comment.

1. Click on the **cell** on which you want to comment. The cell will be selected.

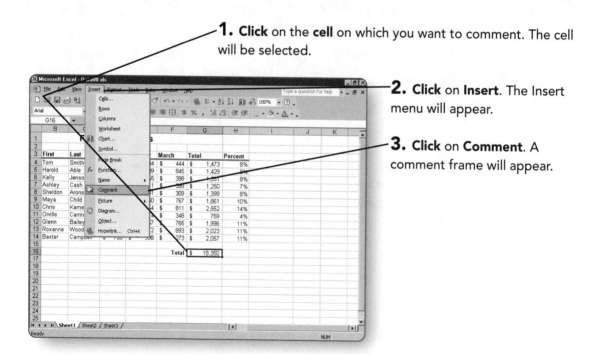

2. Click on **Insert**. The Insert menu will appear.

3. Click on **Comment**. A comment frame will appear.

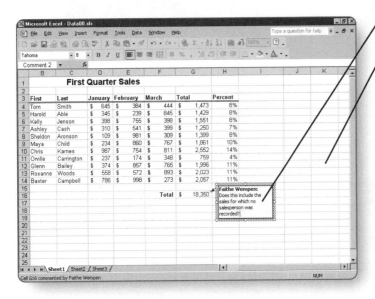

4. **Type** your **comment**.

5. **Click away** from the **comment box**. The comment will be stored, and a triangle will appear in the cell's corner.

Editing a Comment

You can edit a comment at any time, just as you would edit a paragraph or a cell's content.

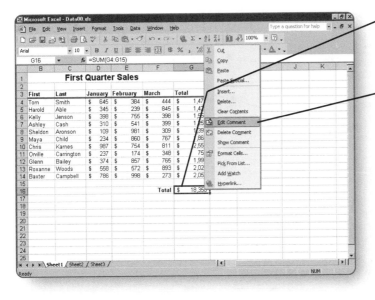

1. **Right-click** on the **cell** with the comment. A shortcut menu will appear.

2. **Click** on **Edit Comment**. The comment box will open for editing.

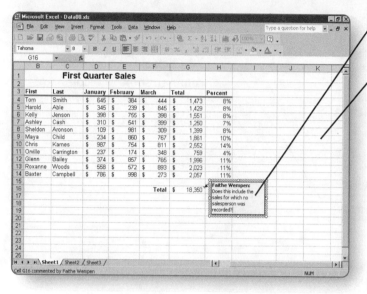

3. Edit the **comment** as needed.

4. Click away from the **comment box**. The changes will be stored.

Deleting a Comment

When the person for whom the comment was intended has read it, he or she will probably want to delete the comment.

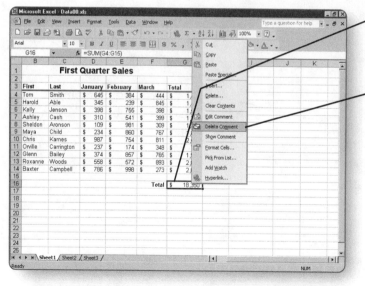

1. Right-click on the **cell** with the comment. A shortcut menu will appear.

2. Click on **Delete Comment**. The comment will be deleted.

Working with Revisions

When more than one person is editing a worksheet, confusion can result over who made what changes. By tracking revisions, you can see at a glance what changes were made and who was responsible.

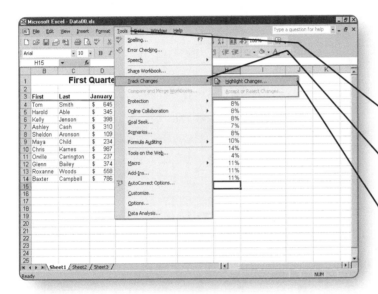

Tracking Revisions

First, you turn on revision tracking in the workbook.

1. **Click** on **Tools**. The Tools menu will appear.

2. **Point** to **Track Changes**. A submenu will appear.

3. **Click** on **Highlight Changes**. The Highlight Changes dialog box will open.

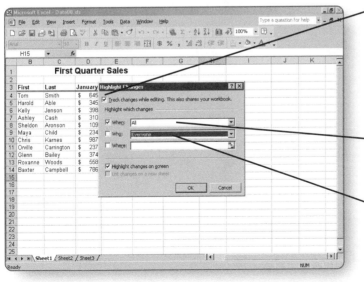

4. **Click** on **Track changes while editing**. A check mark will appear in the check box.

5. (Optional) Do any of the following:

- To track only certain changes, **open** the **When** list and **choose** a **specification**.

- To track changes made by people other than yourself, **open** the **Who** list and **choose Everyone but me**.

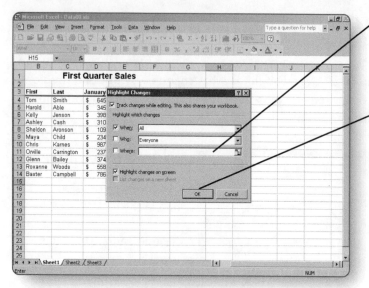

● To track only changes in a certain part of the workbook, **enter** a **range** in the Where box.

6. Click on **OK**. A message will appear that the worksheet will be saved.

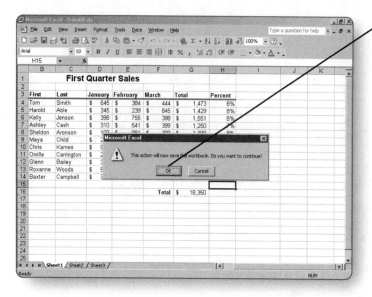

7. Click on **OK**. The worksheet will be saved, and revision tracking will be turned on.

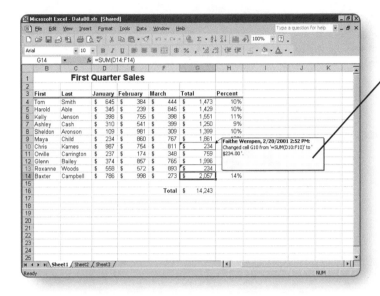

Examining Tracked Revisions

When revision tracking is on, any changes are indicated by a blue triangle in the upper-left corner of a cell. You can see the change by pointing the mouse pointer at the triangle so that a pop-up box appears.

Accepting or Rejecting Tracked Revisions

When you are ready to clean up the workbook after everyone has made their changes, you will want to review all the tracked revisions and accept or reject each one based on its merits.

1. Click on **Tools**. The Tools menu will appear.

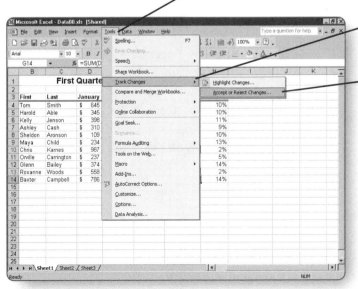

2. Point to **Track Changes**. A submenu will appear.

3. Click on **Accept or Reject Changes**. If you have made changes since the last save, you will be prompted to save the workbook.

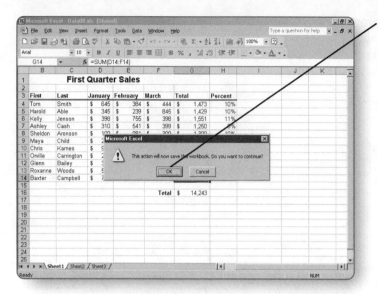

4. Click on **OK**. The Select Changes to Accept or Reject dialog box will open.

5. Do any of the following to specify which changes you want to evaluate:

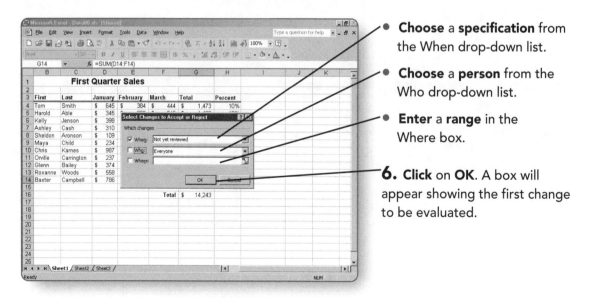

- **Choose** a **specification** from the When drop-down list.

- **Choose** a **person** from the Who drop-down list.

- **Enter** a **range** in the Where box.

6. Click on **OK**. A box will appear showing the first change to be evaluated.

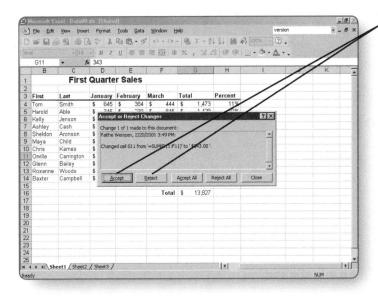

7. Click on **Accept** or **Reject** to keep or discard the change.

8. Repeat step 7 until all the changes have been checked.

When all changes have been checked, the dialog box closes automatically.

Sharing a Workbook

You might have noticed that when you turned on revision tracking, the workbook gained a [Shared] notation in its title bar. Certain features require the workbook to be shared, and revision tracking is one of them.

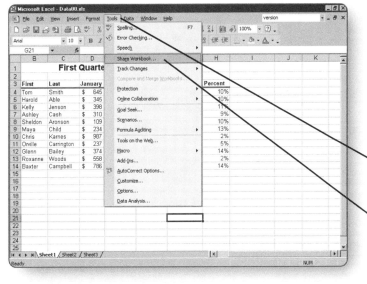

A shared workbook can be edited by more than one person simultaneously in a network environment. You can share or unshare a workbook easily through the Sharing command on the Tools menu.

1. Click on **Tools**. The Tools menu will appear.

2. Click on **Share Workbook**. The Share Workbook dialog box will open.

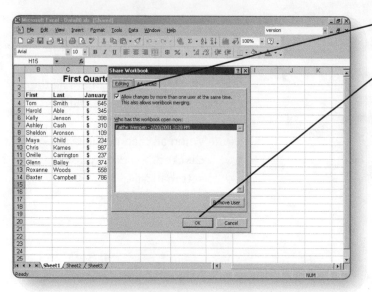

3. **Click** the **check box** to change its setting.

4. **Click** on **OK**. If you are unsharing a workbook, a warning box will appear.

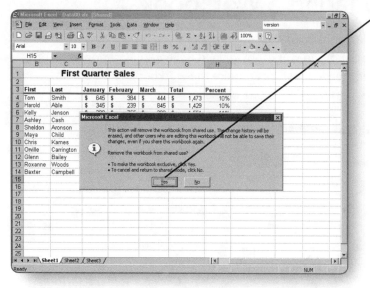

5. **Click** on **Yes**.

Protecting Your Data

If you've invested a great deal of time and effort constructing a worksheet or workbook, you want to be sure that no one can either by accident or, worse, intentionally make unauthorized changes to your data. You can protect your work at the worksheet level by allowing others to view but not to edit the sheet without a password. At the workbook level, you can prevent worksheets from being moved, hidden, or renamed; and windows from being moved, resized, hidden, or closed. Be aware that if you lose the password, you cannot gain access to the files, data, or options you've password protected. Always write down the password and keep it in a secure place.

Protecting a Worksheet

You can protect the integrity of the data in your worksheet by setting up password protection.

1. **Click** on **Tools**. The Tools menu will appear.

2. **Click** on **Protection**. A submenu will appear.

3. **Click** on **Protect Sheet**. The Protect Sheet dialog box will open.

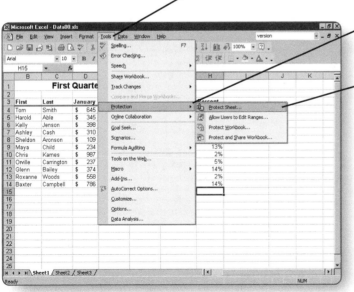

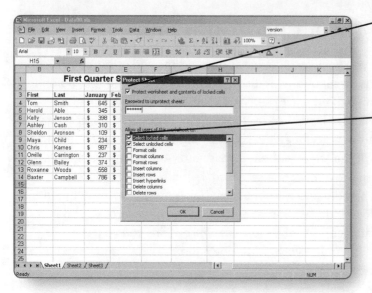

4. Click on the **Protect worksheet and contents of locked cells check box** if it is not already marked.

5. Click on any **check boxes** to change permission settings.

TIP

In most cases the default settings for step 5 work well.

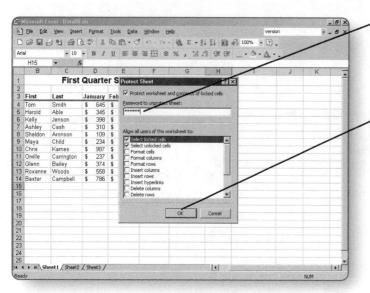

6. Type a **password** in the Password box. A series of asterisks will appear in the box rather than the actual password.

7. Click on **OK**. The Confirm Password dialog box will open.

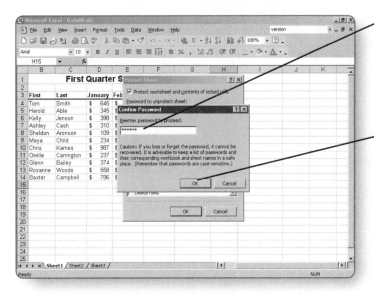

8. Type the **password** again to ensure you typed it correctly the first time. A series of asterisks will appear in the Reenter password to proceed box.

9. Click on **OK**. The Confirm Password dialog box will close.

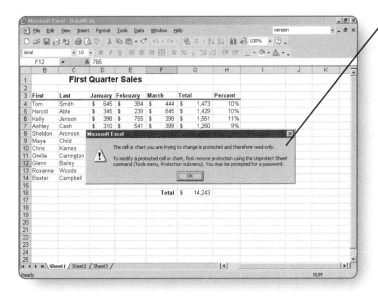

The worksheet can be opened and viewed, but if someone tries to change the data, a prompt will be displayed that says the worksheet is password protected. Without the password, changes cannot be made.

Removing Password Protection from Worksheets

As important as password protection is, sometimes you need to remove it from your worksheets.

1. Click on **Tools**. The Tools menu will appear.

2. Click on **Protection**. A submenu will appear.

3. Click on **Unprotect Sheet**. The Unprotect Sheet dialog box will open.

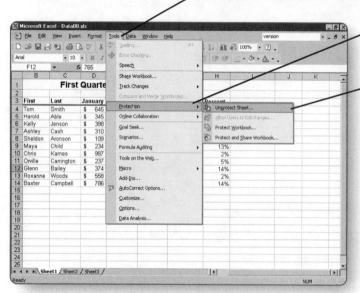

4. Type the **password** in the Password text box.

5. Click on **OK**. The worksheet will be unprotected.

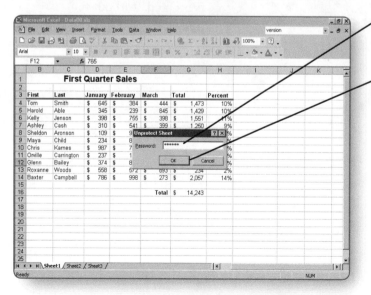

Protecting Your Workbook

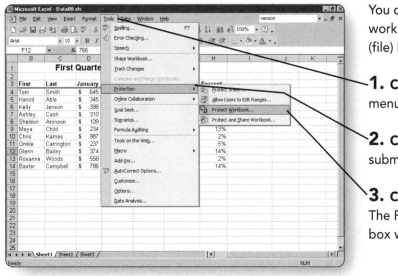

You can also protect your worksheets at the workbook (file) level.

1. **Click** on **Tools**. The Tools menu will appear.

2. **Click** on **Protection**. A submenu will appear.

3. **Click** on **Protect Workbook**. The Protect Workbook dialog box will open.

4. **Click** on **Structure** to put a check mark next to it if there is not already one there. This will prevent the worksheets from being moved, hidden, or renamed, and new sheets from being added.

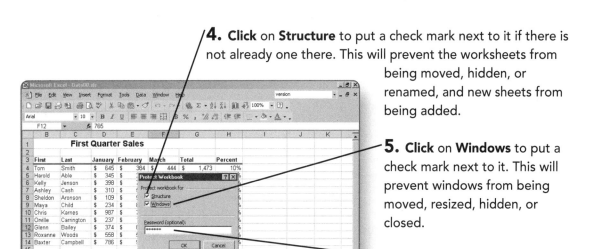

5. **Click** on **Windows** to put a check mark next to it. This will prevent windows from being moved, resized, hidden, or closed.

6. **Type** a **password** in the Password text box.

7. **Click** on **OK**. The Confirm Password dialog box will open.

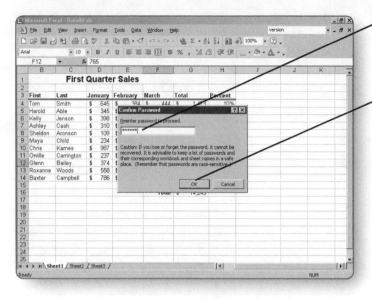

8. Type the **password** again to ensure that you typed it correctly the first time.

9. Click on **OK**. The Confirm Password dialog box will close. Now all commands related to modifying the structure of the workbook or the windows in the workbook will be unavailable (dimmed on the menus) as long as the protection is on.

Removing Password Protection from Workbooks

You must also know how to remove password protection from your workbooks.

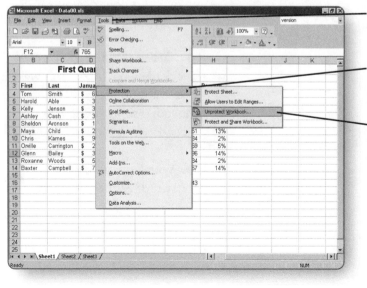

1. Click on **Tools**. The Tools menu will appear.

2. Click on **Protection**. A submenu will appear.

3. Click on **Unprotect Workbook**. The Unprotect Workbook dialog box will open.

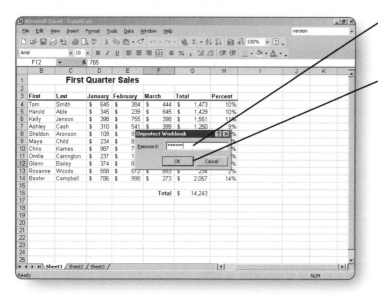

4. **Type** the **password** in the Password text box.

5. **Click** on **OK**. The workbook will be unprotected.

Preventing Your Workbook from Being Opened

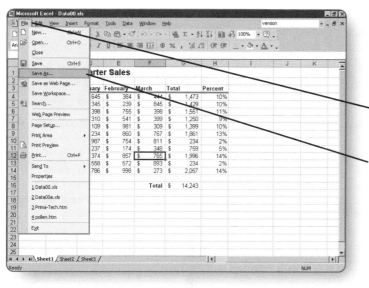

You can also set a password to prevent other people from opening your workbooks altogether.

1. **Click** on **File**. The File menu will appear.

2. **Click** on **Save As**. The Save As dialog box will open.

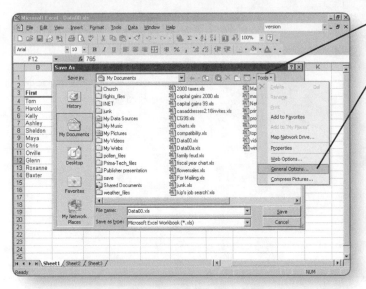

3. Click on **Tools**. A menu will appear.

4. Click on **General Options**. The Save Options dialog box will open.

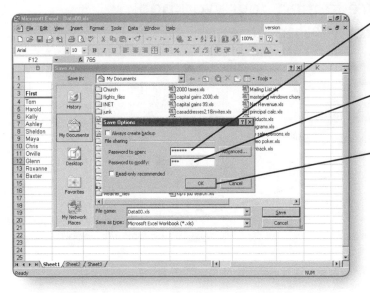

5. Type a **password** in the Password to open text box. Passwords are case-sensitive.

6. Type a **password** in the Password to modify text box.

7. Click on **OK**. The Confirm Password dialog box will open.

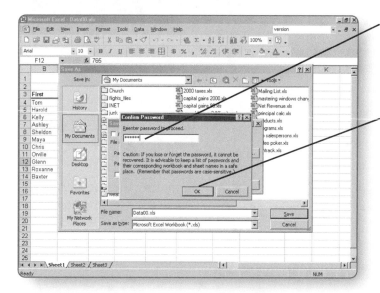

8. Type the read **password** in the Reenter password to proceed text box. This is the password to *read* the file.

9. Click on **OK**. Another Confirm Password dialog box will open.

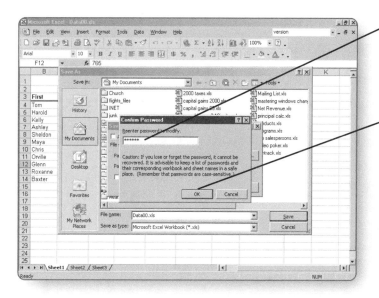

10. Type the modify **password** in the Reenter password to modify text box. This is the password to *modify* the file.

11. Click on **OK**. The Save As dialog box will open.

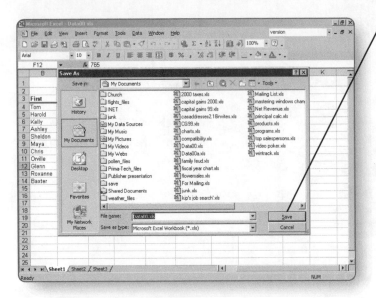

12. **Click** on **Save**. A prompt will appear.

NOTE

To remove the passwords, repeat the same procedure but delete the asterisks from the password boxes.

13. **Click** on **Yes**. The existing workbook will be replaced.

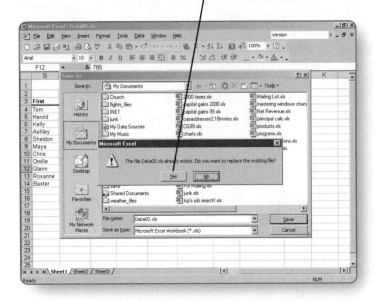

Protecting Only Certain Cells

One common use for protection is to lock users out of certain cells but allow them to change others. This is fairly easy to set up but requires that you know how to protect worksheets.

By default, all cells in the worksheet are locked so that when the worksheet is protected, all cells are protected too. If you want certain cells not to be locked when protection is enabled, you must unlock them first, before enabling protection.

1. Unprotect the **workbook** and the **worksheet** containing the cells, if you have set up protection for them earlier in the chapter.

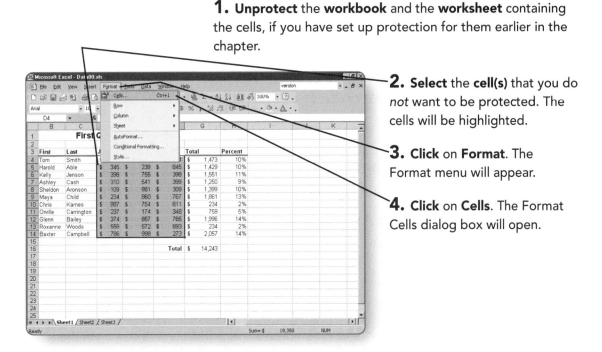

2. Select the **cell(s)** that you do *not* want to be protected. The cells will be highlighted.

3. Click on **Format**. The Format menu will appear.

4. Click on **Cells**. The Format Cells dialog box will open.

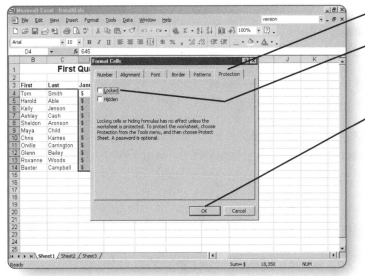

5. Click on the **Protection** tab.

6. Click on the **Locked** check box to clear it if it is not already cleared.

7. Click on **OK**.

8. Repeat steps 2 through 7 for other ranges of cells that you do not want to be protected.

9. Apply protection to the worksheet or workbook, as you learned earlier in the chapter.

The cells that you unlocked will not be protected when the rest of the worksheet is protected.

Part V Review Questions

1. What's a quick way to insert an Excel worksheet grid in a Word document? *See "Creating an Excel Worksheet from within Word" in Chapter 16*

2. What menu command inserts an existing Excel worksheet into a Word document? *See "Inserting an Existing Excel Worksheet into Word" in Chapter 16*

3. What conditions must be met to successfully append data from an Excel worksheet to an existing database table in Access? *See "Appending Excel Data to an Existing Table" in Chapter 17*

4. How can you link an Excel worksheet to an Access database so that both copies change when data is updated in either program? *See "Linking an Excel Worksheet to Access" in Chapter 17*

5. What is a Web Query? *See "Creating a Simple Web Query" in Chapter 18*

6. How can you save a Web query separately from the workbook in which it appears? *See "Saving a Web Query" in Chapter 18*

7. With what formatting does a text hyperlink appear in a cell in Excel? *See "Inserting a Hyperlink" in Chapter 19*

8. What happens when you add interactivity to a worksheet when saving it in Web format? *See "Saving the Worksheet for the Web" in Chapter 19*

9. How can you tell that a comment is attached to a cell? *See "Working with Comments" in Chapter 20*

10. How can you lock all cells in a worksheet except certain ones you specify? *See "Protecting Only Certain Cells" in Chapter 20*

PART VI

Appendixes

A

Installing Excel

Installing Excel really is quick and painless—place the CD in your computer's CD-ROM drive and follow the wizard. In this appendix, you'll learn how to:

- Install Excel on your computer
- Add or remove Office components
- Repair or reinstall Office

Installing the Software

You might have purchased Excel separately or as part of the Office XP suite of programs. Either way, the installation process is similar. This appendix shows the Office XP installation process.

1. Insert the **Office XP CD-ROM** into your computer's CD-ROM drive. The Setup program will start, and the User Information dialog box will open.

> ### NOTE
> If the Setup program does not start automatically, double-click My Computer and then double-click the CD-ROM drive icon.

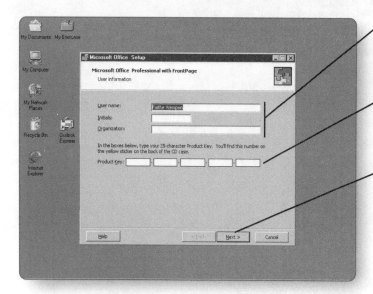

2. Type your **Name**, **Initials**, and **Organization** in the boxes provided.

3. Type the **Product Key** for your CD. It's on a sticker on your Office XP CD case.

4. Click on **Next**. The End User License Agreement will appear.

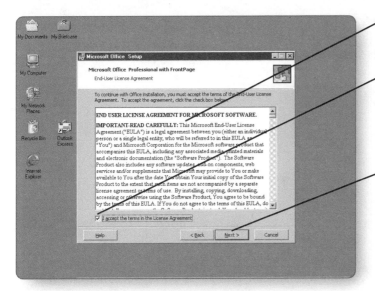

5. Read the **License Agreement**.

6. Click on the **I accept the terms in the License Agreement option button**. The option will be selected.

7. Click on **Next**. The Installation Type controls will appear.

8. (Optional) **Change** the **installation path** in the Install To box if needed.

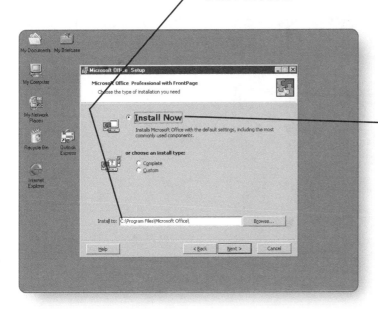

In most cases the default path is fine, but you might need to change it if you don't have enough room on your C: drive.

9a. Click on the **Install Now button**. Use this option to install Office on your computer with the default settings. This is the recommended installation for most users.

OR

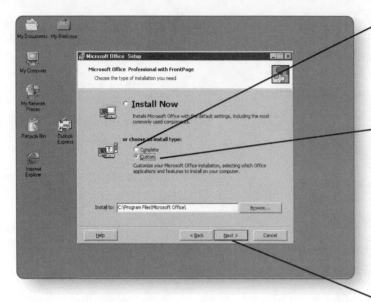

9b. **Click** on the **Complete** button if you want to install every available component.

OR

9c. **Click** on the **Custom** button if you want to choose which components to install or where to install them. The Installation Location dialog box will open. Then see the next section, "Choosing Components," for guidance.

10. **Click** on **Next** to continue. A confirmation screen will appear.

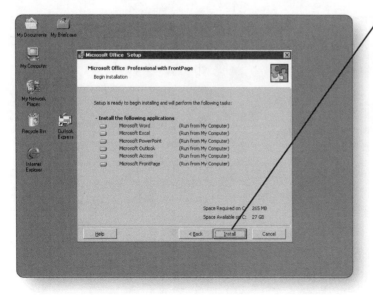

11. **Click** on **Install**. The Setup program will begin copying files.

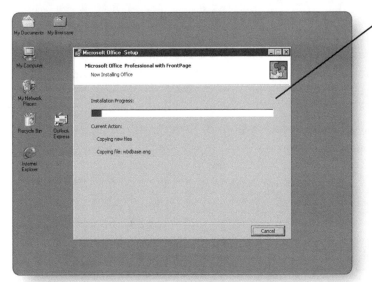

12. Wait while the **Office software** installs on your computer. A confirmation message will appear when it's done.

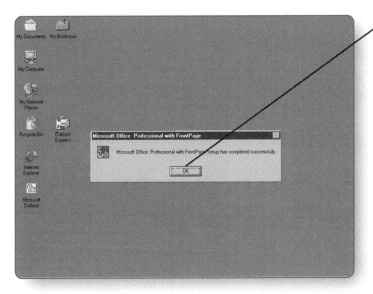

13. Click on **OK** to accept the confirmation.

Choosing Components

If you selected option 9c in the previous section, you have the choice of installing the different programs and components in Office XP.

1. Click on a **check box** to deselect the programs that you don't want to install.

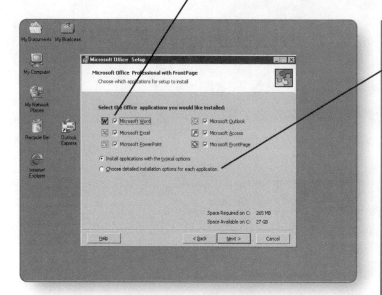

NOTE

There is also an option to fine-tune the custom installation even further by selecting Choose detailed installation options for each application. If you do so, instead of immediately going back to the main installation routine, you see an extra screen on which you can pick specialized options for each application. You'll learn about this interface in the "Adding and Removing Components" section later in this chapter.

2. Go to **step 10** of the preceding procedure.

Working with Maintenance Mode

Maintenance Mode is a feature of the Setup program. Whenever you run the Setup program again, after the initial installation, Maintenance Mode starts automatically. It enables you to add or remove features, repair your Office installation (for example, if files have become corrupted), and remove Office completely.

There are several ways to rerun the Setup program (and thus enter Maintenance Mode):

- Reinsert the Office CD (or Excel CD). The Setup program may start automatically.

- If the Setup program does not start automatically, double-click on the CD icon in the My Computer window. This will either start the Setup program or open a list of files. If it opens a list of files, double-click on Setup.exe.

- From the Control Panel in Windows, click on the Add/Remove Programs button. Then on the Install/Uninstall tab, click on Microsoft Office (or Microsoft Excel) in the list, and finally, click on the Add/Remove button.

After entering Maintenance Mode, choose the button for the activity you want. Each option is briefly described in the following sections.

Adding and Removing Components

You can specify which components you want to install or uninstall.

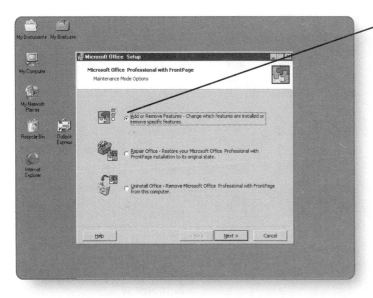

1. Click on the **Add or Remove Features button** in Maintenance Mode. The Features to Install window will appear.

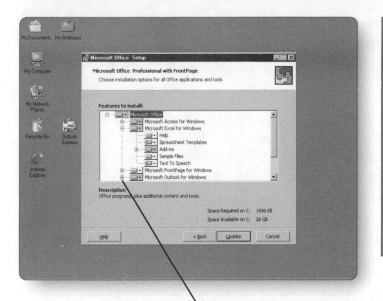

2. Click on a **plus sign (+)** to expand a list of features for a program or category. The features under it will appear.

3. Click on the **down arrow** to the right of the hard drive icon for a feature. A menu of available options for the feature will appear.

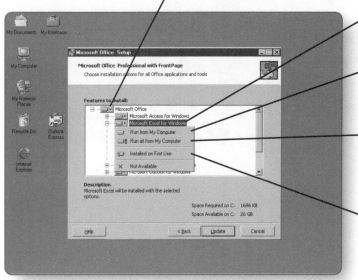

4. Click on the **setting** you want for that feature:

- **Run from My Computer**. The component will be fully installed.

- **Run All from My Computer**. The component and all subcomponents beneath it will be fully installed.

- **Installed on First Use**. The first time you try to access the component, you will be prompted to insert the Office CD to install it.

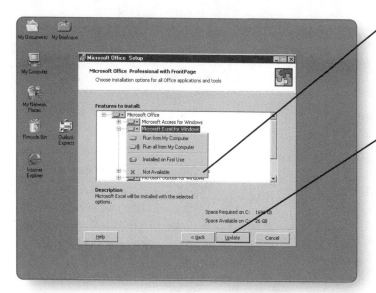

● **Not Available**. The component will not be installed.

5. Repeat steps 2–4 as needed.

6. Click on **Update**. The needed files will be copied or removed.

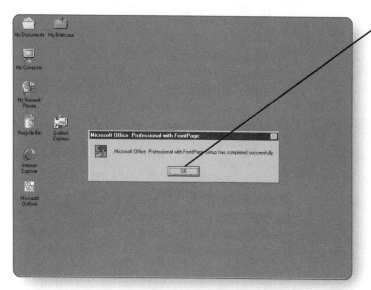

7. Click on **OK** when prompted that the setup has completed.

Repairing or Reinstalling Office

If an Office program is behaving strangely or refuses to work, chances are good that a needed file has become corrupted. But which file? You have no way of knowing, so you can't fix the problem yourself.

If this happens, you can either repair Office or completely reinstall it. Both options are accessed from the Repair Office button in Maintenance Mode.

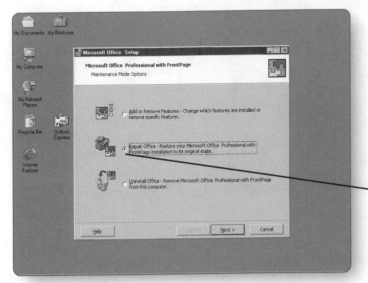

1. Click on the **Repair Office button** in Maintenance Mode.

2a. Click on **Reinstall Office** to repeat the last installation.

OR

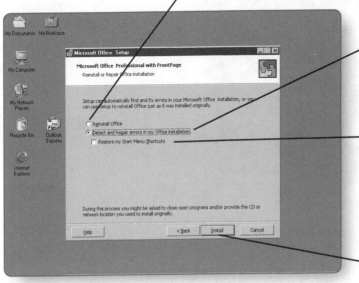

2b. Click on **Detect and Repair errors in my Office installation** to simply fix what's already in place.

3. (Optional) **Click** on the **Restore my Start Menu Shortcuts checkbox** if some of the Office programs do not appear on your Start menu even though they are installed.

4. Click on **Install**. The process will start.

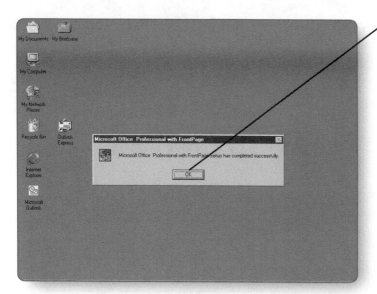

5. Click on **OK** to accept the confirmation that setup has completed successfully.

Removing Office from Your PC

In the unlikely event that you should need to remove Office from your PC completely, click on Remove Office from the Maintenance Mode screen. Then follow the prompts to remove it from your system.

After removing Office, you will probably have a few remnants left behind that the Uninstall routine didn't catch. For example, there will probably still be a Microsoft Office folder in your Program Files folder or wherever you installed the program. You can delete that folder yourself.

B

Using Keyboard Shortcuts

*K*eyboard shortcuts are key combinations you can press as alternatives to choosing menu commands, selecting text or ranges, or applying certain formatting. You may have also noticed keyboard shortcuts listed next to certain menu commands.

For a complete list of keyboard shortcuts, check out the Excel 10 Help system. This appendix provides a few of the most common ones to get you started.

When several keys are listed together, you hold down the first key(s) while tapping the second. For example, if you see Shift+F1, hold down the Shift key, tap F1, and then release Shift.

Working with Menus

Ever wondered about the underlined letters on menu and command names? Those are *selection letters,* and they exist so that you can work with menus and commands using the following shortcuts:

To Do This	Press This
Open a menu	Alt, and then the menu's selection letter
Select a menu command	Up and down arrow keys, and then Enter, or the menu item's selection letter
Close a menu or dialog box	Esc
Show a shortcut menu	Shift+F10

Opening Dialog Boxes

Some of the most common dialog boxes have their own shortcuts, so you can bypass their menu commands:

To Open This Dialog Box	Press This
Save As	Shift+F12 (Ctrl+S also opens it if the file has not been saved before)
Format Cells	Ctrl+1
Print	Ctrl+P
Go To	F5
Open	Ctrl+O
Spelling	F7
Find	Shift+F5

Moving Around in a Worksheet or Workbook

To move the cell cursor around in the workbook, or scroll from one part of the workbook to another, use these shortcuts:

To Move	Press This
One cell in any direction	An arrow key
One screenful in any direction	Alt+ an arrow key
To the edge of the current data region	Ctrl+ an arrow key
To the beginning of the current row	Home
To the top of the worksheet (cell A1)	Ctrl+Home
Up or down one screenful	Page Up or Page Down
To the next cell (right)	Tab
To the previous cell (left)	Shift+Tab

Typing Data into Cells

When you are typing data, you can save time with these:

To Do This	Press This
Start a new formula	= (equal sign)
Start an AutoSum	Alt+= (equal sign)
Start a new line in the same cell	Alt+Enter
Move the insertion point	Arrow keys
Copy the formula from the cell above	Ctrl+' (apostrophe)
Insert today's date	Ctrl+; (semicolon)
Copy the value from the cell above	Ctrl+Shift+" (quotation mark)
Insert the current time	Ctrl+Shift+: (colon)
Cancel entry in a cell	Esc

Applying Number Formats

Many of the number formats (from the Number tab of the Format Cells dialog box) can be applied with keyboard shortcuts:

To Apply This Format	Press This
Number	Ctrl+Shift+!
Date	Ctrl+Shift+#
Currency	Ctrl+Shift+$
Percentage	Ctrl+Shift+%
Time	Ctrl+Shift+@
Exponential	Ctrl+Shift+^
General	Ctrl+Shift+~

Formatting Data

The most popular text formatting commands (bold, italic, and underline) not only have their own toolbar buttons, but their own keyboard shortcuts too:

To Do This	Press This
Turn Bold on and off	Ctrl+B
Turn Italics on and off	Ctrl+I
Turn Underline on and off	Ctrl+U
Open the Format Cells dialog box	Ctrl+1

Getting Help

Find out more about using Excel through the Help system with these keyboard shortcuts:

To Do This	Press This
Summon the Office Assistant	F1
Get What's This? help on-screen elements	Shift+F1

Selecting Ranges of Cells

To select multiple cells, you can use these keyboard shortcuts instead of the usual mouse-dragging method:

To Do This	Press This
Select the entire worksheet	Ctrl+A
Extend the selection	Shift+arrow key
Extend the selection to the end of the row or column	Ctrl+Shift+arrow key
Extend the selection to the bottommost, rightmost cell containing data in the sheet	Ctrl+Shift+End
Extend the selection to cell A1	Ctrl+Shift+Home
Select the column	Ctrl+Spacebar
Extend the selection to the beginning of the row	Shift+Home
Select the row	Shift+Spacebar

Cutting, Copying, and Pasting

Once you've selected a range, you can cut, copy, paste, delete, or clear it. Not only do you have the Edit menu's commands for these actions, and the toolbar buttons, but you also can use these keyboard shortcuts:

To Do This	Press This
Cut the selection	Ctrl+X
Copy the selection	Ctrl+C
Paste the selection	Ctrl+V
Delete the selection	Ctrl+- (hyphen)
Clear the contents of the selection	Delete

Glossary

+	Addition operator.
-	Subtraction operator.
=	Initiates all formulas.
*	Multiplication operator.
/	Division operator.
>	Greater than operator.
<	Less than operator.
B	Not equal to operator.
:	Range operator.

A

Absolute reference. A reference to a cell address that does not change when the formula is moved or copied elsewhere in a worksheet.

Active cell. The selected cell in a worksheet.

Address. A named reference to a cell based on its location at the intersection of a column and row; for example, the cell in the fourth row of the second column has an address of B4.

Alignment. The arrangement of text or an object in relation to the document's margins in Word, a slide's dimensions in PowerPoint, or a cell's edges in Excel. Alignment can be left, right, centered, or justified.

Array. A contiguous set of cells in a worksheet.

AutoFormat. Predefined sets of styles that allow you to quickly apply formatting (color, font, and so on) to your Excel worksheet.

AutoSum. A built-in addition function that allows you to add a row or column of figures using the AutoSum button on the Excel toolbar.

Axis (pl. axes). In a graph, one of two value sets (see also *X axis* and *Y axis*).

B

Bar chart. A type of chart that uses bars of varying lengths to represent values.

Border. A formatting option that places a line around any of the four sides of an object, such as a cell.

C

Cell. The area defined by a rectangle at which a row and a column intersect in an Excel worksheet.

Cell reference. A method of referring to a cell in a formula by listing the location of its row and column intersection.

Chart. Also called a graph. A chart is a visual representation of numerical data.

Circular reference. In a formula, a circular reference indicates that a calculation should return to its starting point and repeat endlessly; a circular reference in a formula results in an error message.

Clip art. Ready-made line drawings that are included with Office in the Clip Art Gallery; these drawings can be inserted into Office documents.

Column. A set of cells running vertically down a worksheet.

Combination chart. A chart that uses more than one style of representing data; for example, bars for one set of data and a line for another set of data. A chart that shows rainfall in a country by month with bars and the average rainfall in the world with a line is an example of a combination chart.

D

Data. Information, which can be either numerical or textual.

Data series. In charts, elements that represent a set of data, such as pie segment, line, or bar.

Data type. The category of numerical data, such as currency, scientific, or percentage.

Desktop. Windows' main work area.

Drag-and-Drop. A feature that allows you to move an object or selected text around an Excel worksheet using your mouse.

E

Equation. See *Formula*.

F

Fill. A function that allows Excel to automatically complete a series of numbers based on an established pattern.

Fill (color). A formatting feature used to apply color or a pattern to the interior of an object, such as a cell.

Fill handle. A block at the lower-right corner of all cells in a worksheet that can be dragged to fill cells as it is dragged across with a pattern of data.

Filter. To hide all data that does not meet specified criteria.

Financial functions. Functions (stored formulas) that are used with money, such as payments and interest rates.

Flip. To turn an object on a page 180 degrees.

Font. A design family of text, also called a typeface.

Footer. Text repeated at the bottom of each page of a document.

Format. To apply settings for font, color, size, and style to data or objects.

Formula. An equation that instructs Excel to perform certain calculations based on numerical data in designated cells.

Formula bar. The location where all data and formulas are entered for a selected cell.

Freezing. In large worksheets, it is sometimes desirable to freeze a portion of the sheet, such as column headings, so that it doesn't scroll off-screen when you move down the page.

Function. A predefined, named formula.

G

General format. A numerical type applied to numbers in cells.

Goal Seek. A feature that allows you to enter the result you want. Excel then determines changes in the formula or data required to obtain the result.

Go To. A feature of Excel that allows you to move quickly to a page or cell of your worksheet based on criteria you provide.

Graphs. See *Chart*.

Greater than. A function that restricts a number result to be higher than a named number.

Gridlines. Lines between the cells of a worksheet. You can specify whether gridlines appear onscreen and whether they appear on printouts.

H

Header. Text repeated at the top of each page of a document.

Hide. A feature of Excel that allows you to temporarily stop displaying designated cells in a worksheet.

I

Icon. In software, a picture representing a feature, such as tool button icon.

IF function. A predefined formula indicating that a result is to occur only if certain criteria are met. For example, you could use this function to indicate that "if the result of a sum is greater than 10, the result should appear in this cell."

J

Justify. To distribute existing text and spaces to completely fill a cell or other defined area from left to right.

L

Label. A descriptive text element added to a chart to help the reader understand a visual element. Also refers to row or column headings.

Landscape. A page orientation that prints a document with the long edge of the paper across the top.

Legend. A definition of the various elements of a chart or graph.

Less than. A predefined function that indicates a result should occur only if a number is less than the specified number.

Logical functions. Functions that are based on the logical consequence of a named set of circumstances, such as the IF . . . THEN function.

M

Macro. A saved series of keystrokes that can be played back to perform an action.

Maps. Representing data in charts with geographical maps rather than traditional chart elements such as bars and lines.

Mathematical functions. Functions that produce mathematical results, such as SUM and AVG.

N

Name definitions. Providing an alternate name for a cell so that you can use that name definition in formulas.

Named ranges. Providing a name for a set of cells so you can use that name in formulas.

O

Object. A picture, map, or other graphic element that you can place in an Excel worksheet.

Office Assistant. A Help feature for Microsoft Office products that allows you to ask questions in standard English sentence format.

Operator. The parts of a formula that indicate an action to be performed, such as addition (+) or division (/).

Optional arguments. A portion of a formula that is not necessary to achieve the result, but that designates an action other than the default. An optional argument to include decimals in a result would include the decimal point and two zeros even if the number doesn't contain cents.

Orientation. The way a document prints on a piece of paper; Landscape prints with the longer side of a page on top, while Portrait prints with the shorter edge at the top.

P

Passwords. A word selected by an Excel user to protect a worksheet; after a sheet is protected, the correct password must be entered to modify that sheet.

Paste. To insert an object or text placed on the Windows Clipboard into a document.

Patterns. Predefined shading and line arrangements used to format cells in a worksheet.

Pie chart. A round chart type in which each pie wedge represents a value.

Plot. The area of a chart where data is drawn using elements such as lines, bars, or pie wedges.

Portrait. A page orientation that results in a document with the shorter edge along the top.

Precedent. Some formulas call on data that is the result of another formula; the precedent is the formula that originally created the data being named in the second formula.

Print area. The portion of a worksheet you designate to print.

Print Preview. A feature that allows you to view a document on your screen appearing as it will when printed.

Protection. To make settings to a worksheet so that only those authorized can modify the worksheet.

R

Range. A collection of cells, ranging from the first named cell to the last.

Recalculation. Used with manual calculation, recalculation is applied to a formula when data has changed to receive the new result.

Redo. A feature of Excel that allows you to repeat an action you have reversed using the Undo feature.

Reference. In a formula, a name or range that refers the formula to a cell or set of cells.

Relative. In a formula, making reference to a cell relative to the location of the cell where the formula is placed; if the formula cell is moved, the cell being referenced changes in relation to the new location.

Rotate. To manipulate an object so that it moves around a 360-degree axis.

Row. A set of cells running from left to right across a worksheet.

S

Save as. To save a previously saved worksheet with a new name or properties.

Scroll bar. A device used to move up and down or left to right in a worksheet to display various portions of it on-screen.

Shading. A gray to black pattern used to format cells in a worksheet.

Sheet. See *Worksheet*.

Sort. To arrange information in a column or row alphanumerically, in ascending or descending order.

Spelling. A feature of Excel that verifies the spelling of words in your worksheets.

Spreadsheet. A software program used to perform calculations on data.

Style. A saved, named set of formatting such as color, size, and font that can be applied to data in a worksheet.

SUM function. A saved, named function of addition that can be applied to cells by typing the term "SUM" in a formula.

Syntax. The structure and order of the functions and references used in a formula.

T

Target cell. The cell where the results of a formula should be placed.

Task pane. The window that appears by default to the right of the work area, providing shortcuts to commonly used commands such as for opening and creating new files.

Template. A predefined set of worksheet formats included with Excel that are useful for quickly generating certain types of documents, such as an invoice.

Text box. A text object that you can create with the drawing feature of Excel to place text anywhere on a chart or worksheet; often used to label elements of a chart or worksheet.

Titles. Names of the elements of a chart.

U

Undo. An Excel feature that allows you to reverse the last action performed.

Unhide. To reveal cells previously hidden in a worksheet.

Unprotect. To remove password safeguards from a worksheet so that anyone can modify the worksheet.

V

Value. Another term for a number.

Variable. Cells that are changed to see what results from that change.

W

What if. A scenario in a formula that supposes certain criteria.

What's This? A part of the Excel Help system; once you select What's This? your cursor changes to a question mark and you can click on any on-screen element to receive an explanation of that element.

Wizard. A feature of Excel that walks you through a procedure step by step; a wizard creates something, such as a chart, using the answers you give to a series of questions.

Workbook. A single Excel file containing a collection of Excel worksheets.

Worksheet. One of several pages in an Excel workbook.

Wrapping. A function that causes text to automatically wrap to the next line when it reaches the right edge of a cell.

X

X axis. In a chart, the axis that runs from left to right.

Y

Y axis. In a chart, the axis that runs from top to bottom.

Index

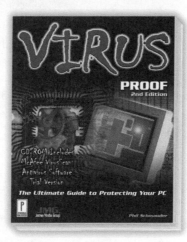
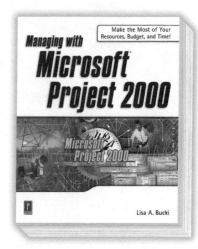

fast&easy web development

PRIMA TECH's *fast&easy* series

Fast Facts, Easy Access

Offering extraordinary value at a bargain price, the *fast & easy* series is dedicated to one idea: To help readers accomplish tasks as quickly and easily as possible. The unique visual teaching method combines concise tutorials and hundreds of screen shots to dramatically increase learning speed and retention of the material. With PRIMA TECH's *fast & easy* series, you simply look and learn.

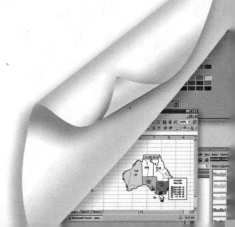